Topics in Unemployment
Insurance Financing

Wayne Vroman

1998

W. E. Upjohn Institute for Employment Research
Kalamazoo, Michigan

Library of Congress Cataloging-in-Publication Data

Vroman, Wayne.
    Topics in unemployment insurance financing / Wayne Vroman.
        p. cm.
    Includes bibliographical references and indexes.
    ISBN 0–88099–194–1 (cloth : alk. paper). — ISBN 0–88099–193–3
(paper : alk. paper)
        1. Insurance, Unemployment—United States—States—Finance.
I. Title.
HD7096.U5V77   1998
368.4'401'0973—dc21   98–41911
                                                                        CIP

The facts presented in this study and the observations and viewpoints expressed are the sole responsibility of the author. They do not necessarily represent positions of the W. E. Upjohn Institute for Employment Research.

Cover design by J. R. Underhill
Index prepared by Nancy Humphreys.
Printed in the United States of America.

CONTENTS

LIST OF TABLES

Acknowledgments

This volume is intended to provide general readers and specialists with information on state unemployment insurance financing. It was written mainly during 1995 and 1996, years of economic expansion and years when state trust fund balances would be expected to be growing at a rapid pace. The book provides a historical overview of recent financing experiences and explores four specialized financing topics: 1) flexible financing, 2) tax-base indexing, 3) alternative methods for financing trust fund debts, and 4) the establishment of state reserve funds.

Several people contributed to the completion of this book. Steve Woodbury at the Upjohn Institute provided encouragement during all phases of the work. Several people at the Unemployment Insurance Service of the U.S. Department of Labor were helpful in providing interpretations, commenting on ideas, and supplying data. Mike Miller and Robert Pavosevich worked closely with me on the empirical analysis of flexible financing as discussed in Chapter 2. Kelleen Worden Kaye worked closely with me on papers that are referenced in Chapters 2 and 5.

Several individuals in the unemployment insurance programs of the states were helpful. While all cannot be cited here, a few deserve special thanks: Charles Mazza in Indiana, Roger Therrien in Connecticut, and Frank Richie in Oregon. However, they do not necessarily agree fully with the interpretation of state experiences which I have given in the text.

Finally, I thank the W. E. Upjohn Institute for the financial support that made this book possible. Opinions expressed in the book are those of the author and do not necessarily reflect the opinions of the Urban Institute or the W. E. Upjohn Institute.

KEY PARAGRAPH ON PG 1, as deciphered by Ann.

This Book explores the financing of state UI programs and it has two general purposes. Thie first purpose is to assess recent financing experiences and to examine UI funding historically. Chapter 1 introductes the reader to alternative financing strategies and discussing fund adequacy. The chapter also reviews key federal statutes that affect UI taxes and state trust funds. The last half of Chatper 1 reviews the history of UI funding with particular emphasis on the funding problems of the 1970s and the 1980s and experiences during the 1990$6A1992 recession. It provides an interprtation of why financing problems were minor during the early 1990s. Finally it reviews the slow pace of post-recession trust fund building during 1993$6A1996 and reports the results of a simulation analysis of potential future funding problems.

The overall conclusion of Chapter 1 is that states will continue to need to maintain large trust fund balances to forestall potential financing problems during a future recession.

The second purpose of this book is to examine specific methods of financing that could be important for states considering changes in their UI tax statutes and/or their approach to trust fund management. Chapters 2 and 3, respectively, study flexible trust fund financing and tax-base indexing. One or both of these financing features are already present in many states. Each feature has implications for the size of a state's desired trust fund balance and for the responsiveness of its revenues during both recessions and sustained economic expansions. Two major conclusions from these chapters should be noted.

1. Flexible financing features such as so-called solvency taxes, while used by many states, have only a limited macro impact. Further, it does not appear that flexible financing has increased significantly in importance over the past 20 years. The prevalence and potential effects of flexible financing have not grown since the late 1980s. Hence, the need for large reserves is no less now than it was before the recession of 1990–1992. Chapter 2 also discusses the impact that flexible financing has on maintaining family income and on providing for the built-in (or automatic) stability of the macroeconomy. Both are traditional UI objectives and both would be impaired by growth in flexible financing.

2. Tax-base indexing (having a tax base that automatically rises with the level of wages) has a number of favorable effects on state UI financing. Especially in states that have an indexed maximum weekly benefit, an indexed tax base helps to ensure that, over the long run, revenues grow at the same rate as benefit payments. Having a balanced growth of revenues and payments helps to ensure that trust fund balances also grow as state economies expand.

Chapters 4 and 5 study two much more specialized methods of financing: debt financing through state bond issues and the establishment of state UI reserve funds. State reserve funds are state-controlled, state-administered, and supported by UI taxes. Both chapters are based on small samples of state experiences: only three states have issued their own bonds to repay UI debts, and only four have established state reserve funds. Two major conclusions from these chapters are that

1. Bond financing has disadvantages as well as advantages when compared with debt financing with loans from the U.S. Treasury; the choice between the two involves much more than a simple comparison of interest rates.

2. For states with reasonably large UI trust fund balances, the creation of a state reserve fund allows for a proactive use of reserves, such as financing worker training and/or supplementing the administrative budgets of employment security agencies.

Finally, Chapter 6 offers conclusions and some policy recommendations.

Two broad conclusions of this study should be emphasized. First, states continue to need to rely heavily on advance funding, or forward funding, to finance recession-related drawdowns of UI trust fund reserves. The experiences of the 1990–1992 recession do not indicate the scale of potential drawdowns during a future recession. Prudent state policy would maintain UI trust fund balances that meet standard actuarial definitions of fund adequacy. The federal government could help the states in this area by providing active guidance on trust fund adequacy. Second, individual states continue to experiment with UI financing arrangements. Some of these experiments are worth emulating, while others should be avoided. On balance, tax-base indexing merits widespread adoption, as does the use of reserve funds by states with high levels of reserves. The risks in relying on flexible financing should be recognized. At the same time, issuing state bonds to finance trust fund debts also entails risks. Ultimately, of course, individual states will decide on the desirability of each UI financing arrangement.

1 The History of State UI Financing

Unemployment insurance is an important and long-standing social insurance program in the United States. Created by the Social Security Act of 1935, UI pays benefits to 15 to 20 million claimants in most years, benefits financed mainly by payroll taxes levied on covered employers. Employer contributions deposited into state trust fund accounts at the U.S. Treasury are the source for cash benefit payments to claimants.

Unemployment insurance is often described as having three primary objectives. First among these is to "alleviate the hardships that result from loss of wage income during unemployment" (Haber and Murray 1966, p. 26). The cash benefits paid provide partial wage-loss replacement and help to maintain the income and purchasing power of eligible unemployed persons and their families. Payments typically are made to individuals who have lost jobs through no fault of their own, that is, those on layoff, and benefits are received for temporary periods. The second objective is to help stabilize the macroeconomy through the maintenance of aggregate consumer purchasing power during recessions, when the production of goods and services declines. The third objective is to help stabilize employment by experience-rating of individual covered employers. Employers who, through layoffs and other job separations, cause large payments in UI benefits then pay higher UI taxes than employers who initiate fewer job separations.

THE LEGAL AND INSTITUTIONAL FRAMEWORK

In the United States, unemployment insurance features a blend of federal and state responsibilities. The states administer benefit payments and tax collections and determine most of the statutory provisions related to those activities. There are also federal responsibilities, the most important of which charges the U.S. Secretary of Labor with ensuring the prompt and efficient administration of the UI program.

Three tiers of benefit payments are provided. Tier one is the regular benefit program, which operates continuously and pays benefits for up to 26 weeks in most states. Regular UI is financed by state-level employer taxes. The second tier is the federal-state extended benefit (or EB) program, which may pay up to an additional 13 weeks of benefits. This program, activated when states reach set rates of unemployment, is financed equally by state and federal UI taxes. The third tier, temporary benefits, becomes available through special federal legislation during recessions. The most recent temporary program, Emergency Unemployment Compensation, paid benefits from November 1991 through April 1994. Traditionally, such benefits have been financed completely from federal funds. This book is concerned with state-level financing, that is, the financing of regular UI benefits plus half of the EB benefits.

A unique feature of state UI financing in the United States is the reliance on experience-rating to set contribution rates for covered employers. Benefit payments are charged against individual employers, and higher payouts result in increased state UI taxes.

UI programs try to achieve their three main objectives through statutory provisions and administrative procedures that specify coverage, employer contributions, benefit eligibility, and trust fund management practices. Coverage of wage and salary workers is nearly universal, encompassing those who work for private employers, state and local governments, and nonprofit organizations.

Regular state UI benefits for eligible unemployed workers are typically available for up to 26 weeks. Most recipients are on temporary or permanent layoff, but others (job leavers and unemployed labor force reentrants) may also qualify for benefits under certain circumstances. Weekly benefit rates reflect past earnings, typically earnings from the highest calendar quarter of a 12-month "base period" that ended before the onset of unemployment. In many states, base-period earnings determine the maximum duration of benefits and the weekly amount.[1]

States also set the employer payroll taxes that finance UI programs. The original authorizing legislation that established UI (Title IX of the Social Security Act of 1935) provided for a federal unemployment tax (FUT) of 3.0 percent to be levied on the payrolls of covered employers. Also authorized, however, was a tax credit offset mechanism that allowed employers to take credit for up to 90 percent of the FUT (2.7 percent of payrolls) if the state established an acceptable UI program. One requirement for having an acceptable program was that a state must establish an approved mechanism for taxing covered employers according to their experiences in paying UI benefits. The U.S. Secretary of Labor is responsible for judging the acceptability of each state's UI system of experience-rating; the Secretary's responsibilities are discussed later in this chapter. In states with an acceptable experience-rating, employers could pay UI taxes into their state's UI trust fund at a rate of less than 2.7 percent but receive the full 2.7 percent FUT credit offset. That arrangement provided a strong financial incentive for states to establish acceptable programs, and all states did this in the late 1930s.

The other 10 percent of the original 3.0 percent FUT (or 0.3 percent of payrolls) remained a federal tax paid into separate federal trust fund accounts. The proceeds of this tax were originally used to finance UI program administration and the activities of state employment services. The federal component of UI taxes was (and continues to be) levied at a single flat rate.

Experience-rating applies to the state taxes that finance regular state UI benefits and the state's share of EB benefits. Originally, UI taxes were levied on total covered payrolls, but in 1940 the taxable wage base was set at the first $3,000 of annual employee earnings, to correspond to the taxable wage base under the Old Age and Survivors Insurance (OASI), or social security, program.

The state UI trust funds that receive each state's UI taxes are maintained at the U.S. Department of the Treasury. Trust fund balances are invested in the U.S. government debt and earn interest income for the states.

When a state's trust fund becomes depleted, there also are provisions governing whether it may borrow from the U.S. Treasury. Borrowing was widespread during the mid 1970s and again during the early to mid 1980s. Since the early 1980s, the loans have carried interest charges if such debt is outstanding for more than a year. (The federal statutes governing UI loans and debt repayment are discussed later in this chapter and in Chapter 4. See also Miller, Pavosevich, and Vroman [1997] and Vroman [1990]).

Such statutory and institutional arrangements governing federal and state UI taxes have persisted from the 1930s to the present. The

partial control over the use of UI tax revenues. Chapter 5 reviews the performance of such funds in three states.

4.   States that secure loans from the U.S. Treasury must meet debt repayment requirements. Chapter 4 studies state experiences in direct bond issues as an alternative to the use of Treasury loans.

Forty-one of 53 UI programs operated with tax bases above $7,000 in 1996. However, the 1996 tax bases exceeded $10,000 in only 20 states and exceeded $20,000 in just five states. For comparison, the 1996 Old Age, Survivors, and Disability Insurance (OASDI; social security) tax base was $62,700. Due to generally low taxable wage bases, taxable payrolls represented only 35.2 percent of UI covered payrolls in 1995. The higher tax bases are found in the 18 programs with indexed taxable wage bases. Chapter 3 explores the link between the UI tax base and state trust fund adequacy.

In more than half the states, taxes flow into state trust funds from two distinct sources. The first (and largest) source is the tax determined by the state's system of experience-rating individual employers. States typically use three factors to set experience-rated taxes. First, most states have a set of tax rate schedules with higher rates in effect when trust fund balances are lower. Second, such states use an indicator of the overall trust fund balance on a specific computation date (most often June 30th) to determine which rate schedule will be used in the coming year. Third, these states assign rates to individual employers by using an indicator based on each employer's experience in causing the payment of benefits. Higher payout rates lead to higher tax rates. This institutional arrangement for taxation has been present since the founding of the state UI programs.

The second source of funds is often called a "solvency tax," and it takes effect only when the state's trust fund has reached such a low level that there is serious risk of insolvency. A wide variety of solvency taxes now exists in the states. Some are levied at a single flat rate on all employers, while others use an experience indicator to determine individual employer rates. Some states have a single solvency rate, while others have a schedule of such taxes with progressively higher tax rates applying as the trust fund balance reaches progressively lower thresholds.

Solvency taxes are part of a larger set of UI financing arrangements collectively known as "flexible financing." Flexible financing may also extend to a state's UI tax base and to its benefit payments. An advantage of flexible financing, according to its proponents, is that the state can then operate with a lower trust fund balance than it could if it relied on the traditional method of UI financing. Flexible financing is examined in some detail in Chapter 2.

FUNDING STRATEGIES AND CONCEPTS

Advance Funding

The revenues that finance state UI programs come mainly from payroll taxes on covered employers. Taxes are deposited into state UI trust fund accounts at the U.S. Treasury. These accounts are the source for benefit payments.

The funding strategy followed by state UI programs is usually characterized as "advance funding" or "forward funding." (A second funding strategy, "pay-as-you-go," is discussed later in this section.) Trust fund balances are built up before recessions, drawn on during recessions, and then rebuilt during the subsequent recoveries. The funding arrangement implies that the program acts as an automatic stabilizer of economic activity, that it makes larger benefit payments than tax withdrawals during recessions and larger tax withdrawals than benefit payments during economic expansions.

This characterization of advance funding does not accurately describe developments during the recessions of the mid 1970s and the early 1980s. Pre-recession trust fund balances were not large in several states and were too low to pay UI benefits to all eligible claimants. Widespread, large-scale, and persistent state borrowing took place during both recessions. However, during the 1990–1992 downturn, state trust fund reserves were generally sufficient to meet demands for benefit payments without states having to resort to large-scale borrowing.

The adequacy of a state's reserves during a recession depends upon four factors: 1) the absolute size of the trust fund balance at the start of the downturn, 2) the size of the state's economy, 3) the recession-related demand for benefits, that is, the severity and duration of the recession, and 4) the speed and size of response of taxes (and possibly the response of UI benefits) when reserves are drawn down. A concept that has proved useful for assessing state trust fund adequacy is the "reserve ratio multiple" (RRM; also called the "high-cost multiple").

The reserve ratio multiple is an actuarial construct that incorporates the first three of the preceding four factors (the trust fund balance, the size of the state economy, and the benefit payout rate). The denominator in the RRM is the highest-cost benefit payout period in the state's history, measured as total benefit payouts over a 12-month period and expressed as a percentage of covered wages for that period. The interstate range of high-cost percentages extends from a low of 1.04 percent (in South Dakota between January and December 1964) to a high of 4.37 percent (in Rhode Island between January and December 1975). The highest-cost period for the United States as a whole was 2.22 percent (between January and December 1975).

The numerator of the RRM, termed the reserve ratio, is the year-end trust fund balance divided by covered wages for the year and expressed as a percentage. As the ratio of these two ratios, the reserve ratio multiple is thus a measure whose numerator incorporates information on the UI trust fund balance and on the scale of a state's economy (as approximated by covered wages), while the denominator is a measure of risk (the highest previous 12-month payout rate). In the past, some have advocated that states build trust fund reserves to levels that produce RRMs of 1.5, that is, levels equal to 18 months of benefits paid out at the historically highest payout rate.

As a measure of trust fund adequacy, the RRM has its critics. Many analysts consider the 1.5 value too conservative a standard and that a prudent state could function with a much lower trust fund balance and run little or no risk of fund insolvency.

Two specific criticisms of the RRM are often voiced. First, the high-cost period in the denominator is often so far in the past (January–December 1964 for South Dakota) that it may no longer be a relevant indicator of the maximum payout risk. Second, the RRM is a static concept and does not adequately account for the dynamic response of taxes (and perhaps benefits) when trust funds are depleted. A quick response can permit a state to function successfully with a smaller trust fund than that suggested by an RRM of 1.5.

The second variant can be called "ad-hoc pay-as-you-go." It relies on a legislated response mechanism when the trust fund is low or in deficit. There is no substantial written literature that advocates this strategy, but it could be inferred if a state satisfied specific conditions: i.e., 1) limited reserve build-up and a low RRM after a long period of economic expansion and 2) the absence of automatic tax and benefit response features. In effect, ad-hoc pay-as-you-go funding would address the financing problem at the point in time when the problem is most pressing.

When the primary objectives of state UI programs are considered, the rationale for pay-as-you-go strategies seems questionable. Both the temporary replacement of lost earnings for individuals and the automatic macro stabilizing effect of UI are weakened if benefits are reduced during a recession. It would also seem questionable to increase employer taxes in the midst of a recession, when profits are already depressed. However, the strategy does offer a rationale for operating with lower trust fund balances than advanced funding requires. The automatic variant of the pay-as-you-go strategy, flexible financing, is examined further in Chapter 2.

In selecting the desired target level for a state's trust fund, the biggest unknown is the size of the trust fund outflow to expect in future recessions. There is no easy answer to this question. Selecting the highest-ever past rate of outflows may not be useful. For example, decreases in manufacturing's share of total employment and declining unionization are now widespread throughout the United States. Both unionized and nonunionized manufacturing workers and other unionized workers claim UI benefits at above-average rates. This may presage lower benefit-cost rates in the future. On the other hand, relying solely on the experiences of the past 10 years likely means relying on too short an interval.

The example of Michigan may be instructive for reviewing high costs in past periods. During the 10 years from 1987 through 1996, Michigan's highest 12-month benefit-cost rate was 1.90 percent, in 1991. However, the past 10 years have been unusual in Michigan, a state that continues to rely heavily on the cyclically volatile automobile industry. During the 50 years from 1947 to 1996, there were seven years when the cost rate was higher than 1.90 percent. The five years with the highest percentage cost rates were 1982 (3.72), 1958 (3.69),

1975 (2.87), 1980 (2.55), and 1961 (2.20). Each year is a recession year with a higher payout rate than in 1991. Thus, the highest-ever cost rate for Michigan was 3.72 percent, while the highest three-year average for the past 20 years (1977 through 1996) was 2.75 percent. Both cost rates are considerably higher than 1.90 percent, the highest cost rate for 1987 through 1996. It seems clear that experiences covering more than 10 years are needed to assess the likely recession-related costs for a state.

Reserve ratio multiples as measures of adequacy imply large absolute levels of trust fund balances. The 1996 year-end trust fund balances required in Michigan, based on a high-cost multiple of 1.0 combined with each of the preceding three high-cost rates (3.72, 2.75, and 1.90) were $4.0 billion, $3.0 billion, and $2.1 billion, respectively. The state's actual balance was $1.8 billion. Because the absolute balance is such a large number (nearly $2.0 billion), some might misinterpret the degree of adequacy that it represents. Michigan's economy had roughly $110 billion in covered wages in 1996. A 2.0 percent cost rate in 1997 would represent a one-year outflow from its trust fund of about $2.2 billion. It is not difficult to imagine a situation in which the $1.8 billion trust fund balance would drop to zero during the second year of a recession.

MAJOR HISTORICAL DEVELOPMENTS
IN STATE TRUST FUNDS

Aggregate trust fund balances totaled $38.6 billion at the end of 1996. The aggregate balance had been $36.9 million at the end of 1989, just before the 1990–1992 recession. While the dollar value of the 1996 balance was larger by $1.76 billion, it represented a smaller percentage of total covered wages and a lower reserve ratio multiple than the 1989 balance. The national RRM had been 0.87 at the end of 1989 but was only 0.64 seven years later.

This section reviews the history of UI financing, with particular attention to the problems of the mid 1970s and early 1980s. Developments during the 1990s are discussed in the following section (p. 21), along with an assessment of UI trust fund adequacy at the end of 1996.

Beginning with the establishment of UI in the late 1930s, there are four distinct periods of trust fund financing. Sustained and large accumulations occurred during the earliest years. These accumulations were the result of lower benefit costs than originally anticipated when UI was established and of the effects of full employment during World War II. The aggregate reserve ratio (the total net reserves as a percentage of covered wages) reached its all-time peak, 10.4 percent, at the end of 1945. Modest absolute growth in reserves continued through the end of 1948, when the national total of $7.60 billion represented 7.91 percent of covered payrolls.

The trust fund accumulations of these years were also the product of the strong macroeconomy associated with World War II. Aggregate benefit payments, which had averaged about 1.5 percent of covered payrolls during 1938–1940, averaged only about 0.5 percent of payrolls during 1941–1945, with especially low payout rates during 1943 and 1944. Despite large reductions in average tax rates (from 2.69 percent of payroll in 1938 to 1.50 percent in 1945), tax revenues exceeded benefits in every year through 1945.

The second period can be called "the long slide." During the 32 years from 1948 to 1979, growth in UI trust fund reserves lagged substantially behind growth in the economy. The aggregate reserve ratio declined sharply, from 7.91 percent in 1948 to 0.91 percent in 1979. Losses in reserves were concentrated during recessions, but accumulations during economic expansions were generally modest. Consequently, the aggregate reserve ratio was lower before each recession than it had been before the previous recession. Even during the long expansion of the 1960s, the growth in net reserves was no faster than that of covered payrolls. Thus, the reserve ratio, which had been 3.57 percent at the end of 1959, was 3.46 percent at the end of 1969, despite the fact that aggregate reserves had nearly doubled, growing from $6.67 billion in 1959 to $12.64 billion in 1969.

Because state reserves were so large at the start of the 1948–1979 period, the decline in reserves did not present financing problems for many states until the mid 1970s. Alaska, Michigan, and Pennsylvania were the only states that borrowed from the U.S. Treasury to finance benefits during the 1950s and 1960s. These loans were fully repaid by the late 1960s.

Substantial drawdowns of state trust funds occurred in the early 1970s. The first states to require loans were Connecticut, Vermont, and Washington during 1972–1974, with reductions in defense-related procurement causing especially high unemployment in Connecticut and Washington.

Large-scale borrowing from the U.S. Treasury first became widespread in 1975 as the 1974–1975 recession caused financing problems for many states. Nearly half of all UI programs required loans during 1975–1978, and aggregate borrowing totaled $5.5 billion. Moreover, the post-1975 recovery was not robust enough to restore trust fund balances fully by the end of the 1970s. Several debtor states repaid their loans slowly, and aggregate reserves totaled only $8.58 billion at the end of 1979. This balance was about $2.5 billion less than it had been at the end of 1973 and $4.1 billion less than at the end of 1969. The reserve ratio at the end of 1979 was only 0.91 percent, roughly one-fourth of the reserve ratio at the end of 1969 (3.46 percent) and only about one-eighth of the reserve ratio at the end of 1945 (7.91 percent).

The second period of substantial state borrowing occurred during the back-to-back recessions of the early 1980s. Because state programs entered the 1980–1982 recessions with historically low reserves, borrowing was even more widespread and on a larger scale during the early 1980s than during the 1970s. Between 1980 and 1987, total borrowing was $24.2 billion, with four states—Illinois, Michigan, Ohio and Pennsylvania—responsible for over 60 percent of the total. Aggregate reserves reached a low point at the end of 1983, when the nationwide total was actually negative: −$5.8 billion. Debtor states brought in major tax increases and reduced benefits as they attempted to restore trust funds to adequate levels.

The six years starting in 1984 witnessed large-scale trust fund building, with the states adding more than $42 billion to net reserves, about $7.0 billion per year. This yielded an aggregate balance of $36.9 billion at the end of 1989. Despite the growth in absolute reserve balances, the aggregate reserve ratio in 1989 was only 1.92 percent, slightly more than half of its 1969 level of 3.46 percent. Taking the highest-ever national cost rate (2.22 percent during calendar-year 1975) as the high-cost rate gives a nationwide reserve ratio multiple of 0.87 for 1989; this 1989 multiple has not been reached during the 1990s.

Thus, 1989 marks the end of the third historical period, a second period of substantial trust fund accumulations. While the absolute increases in reserves were impressive, the indicators of relative size did not grow nearly so dramatically. Compared to the 1948 reserve ratio of 7.91 percent, the 1989 reserve ratio of 1.92 percent was about one-fourth as large. Nonetheless, during the 1990–1992 recession, states did not need the large-scale loans they had required during 1974–1978 and again during 1980–1987. Unlike the 1970s and 1980s, only seven states borrowed during 1990–1995, and just two had loans that were "large," i.e., more than 1 percent of covered wages.

Another contrast to earlier recessions is that the 1990–1992 downturn was unusually mild in most areas of the country. As a consequence, the drawdowns on trust fund balances were unusually small. Net reserves decreased by $11.0 billion during 1990–1992, compared with $14.4 billion during 1980–1983. We shall return to this topic later.

A third contrast between the 1990s and the 1980s is that there was no substantial trust fund building during the economic expansion of 1993–1996. The four-year increase in aggregate net reserves was only $12.8 billion, or $3.2 billion per year. This rate of accumulation is less than half the annual rate during 1984–1989. As a consequence, the aggregate reserve ratio for the economy only grew from 1.38 percent at the end of 1992 to 1.43 percent at the end of 1996, and the RRM increased only from 0.54 to 0.64. On a relative basis, national reserves were about three-quarters as adequate at the end of 1996 as they had been at the end of 1989.

The slow pace of reserve accumulation characteristic of the 1990s marks this decade as the fourth period in the history of UI trust fund reserves. Compared with the long period from 1948 to 1970, the pattern of recession-related reserve losses and subsequent accumulations in the 1990s is broadly similar, but it is based on a single recession-recovery episode. Trust funds declined during the recession but were not restored to pre-recession levels during the subsequent economic expansion. A repetition of this recession-recovery pattern could lead to renewed large-scale borrowing. Since reserve ratios were so much more modest at the end of 1989 compared with those of 1948, the next recession may entail the large-scale borrowing that occurred during the 1970s and 1980s. The slow reserve accumulations during 1993–1996 and the potential for large-scale borrowing during a future recession are discussed in the next section of this chapter.

State borrowing from the U.S. Treasury is not necessarily to be avoided at all times. Temporary loans for cash-flow purposes, because of differing seasonal patterns of tax revenues and benefit payments, can occasionally occur without causing large or persistent indebtedness. Interest-free seasonal cash-flow loans have always been available to the states. Loans secured but fully repaid before September 30th of the same year are interest-free.

Since the early 1980s, however, longer-term indebtedness has carried interest charges. If the debt is outstanding on January 1st of two consecutive years and has not been fully repaid by November 10th of the second year, an automatic debt repayment process comes into effect. On January 1st of the following year, 0.3 percent is added to the federal part of each employer's UI tax obligation, i.e., 1.1 percent rather than 0.8 percent on the first $7,000 of earnings for each employee. The proceeds of the 0.3 percent penalty tax are used to repay the oldest part of a state's debt. Even higher penalty tax rates apply in later years.

Because federal UI penalty taxes are levied at a flat rate, a state may prefer to make voluntary repayments with experience-rated state UI taxes. These must be levied as new tax obligations (not as withdrawals from the state's UI trust fund), and their yield must at least equal the yield of the federal penalty tax. Voluntary repayment can also be accomplished through a special assessment levied on top of regular employer state UI taxes.

Before 1981, debt repayment provisions differed from current provisions in several ways. Two especially important contrasts should be noted: 1) loans did not carry interest charges and 2) automatic debt repayment through mandatory FUT penalty taxes was suspended by emergency federal legislation. In short, debt burdens before 1981 were lighter than at present. That the increase in the cost of indebtedness helps shape state attitudes towards debt is shown by their debt repayment behavior.[7] Debts incurred in the 1970s were repaid slowly, but post-1982 debts were repaid rapidly. Post-1982 debts were often held for such short periods that no interest was due.

The faster pace of debt repayment since 1982 partly reflects the states' willingness to cut benefit payments while their economies are still in recession. Thus, one consequence of trust fund inadequacy is that legislation designed to improve fund adequacy typically includes benefit reductions as well as tax increases.[8] Another reason to encourage the states to build large trust funds is to avoid recession-related benefit reductions.

To help illustrate the link between a standard indicator of trust fund adequacy and state borrowing, Table 1-1 displays summary data from recent recessions of the 1970s, 1980s, and 1990s. The top panel of Table 1-1 shows reserve ratio multiples for the ends of the years just before the onset of each of the four most recent recessions, plus the multiples at the end of 1996. The back-to-back recessions of 1980 and 1981–1982 are treated as a single, very serious recession. The top panel vividly illustrates the loss of reserve adequacy since the end of 1969. In 1969, only one state had an RRM below 1.0, and 35 had multiples of 1.5 or larger. By 1979, 10 states had multiples that were negative and 12 had multiples below 0.50, while only 2 states had multiples of 1.5 or larger.

In Table 1-1, note how the reserve accumulations of 1984–1989 changed the distribution of multiples. While only 4 states had multiples above 1.5 in 1989, 17 others had multiples between 1.0 and 1.49. The number of multiples that fell below 0.50 decreased from 22 in 1979 to 9 in 1989. When the multiples in the individual states are examined, the increase in the aggregate RRM between 1979 and 1989 (from 0.41 to 0.87) shows the expected pattern.

The top panel of Table 1-1 also shows the decline in the distribution of state RRMs between 1989 and 1996. In both years, nearly all programs had multiples in the range of 0.0 to 1.49. In 1996, however, eight fewer states had multiples between 1.0 and 1.49 (9 versus 17), while while two more had multiples between 0.5 and 0.99 (24 versus 22) and seven more had multiples between 0.0 and 0.49 (16 versus 9). More states had low multiples at the start of 1997 than seven years earlier.

Although it may be obvious to most readers, there is a strong association between the level of a state's RRM before a recession and the likelihood of borrowing during a recession. The lower part of Table 1-1 illustrates this association with data on state borrowing from 1974–1979, 1980–1987, and 1990–1995. The first row for each period gives the initial distribution of state RRMs before the onset of the recession.

SOURCE: All data on trust fund reserves and loans are from the U.S. Department of the [...]

[...] Social programs are those of the 50 states plus the District of Columbia, and Puerto Rico. The Virgin Islands are excluded from the table.

[...] "Loss" years are defined as the total borrowing over the indicated period. Values are shown as negative of amount of total payouts for a single year [...] in the periods indicated: 1975, 1984, and 1991, respectively.

The second row shows how many states in each interval needed any loan during the years indicated. The third row shows the number of states needing large loans, "large" being defined as total borrowing during the entire period equal to 1 percent or more of the total covered wages for one year in the period indicated.

During 1974–1979, 24 programs borrowed and 15 needed large loans. The probability of a state needing a loan and needing a large loan was much higher for states with low initial reserve ratio multiples. All five states with multiples below 0.50 borrowed, and all five needed large loans during 1974–1979. Of the 21 states with initial RRMs of 1.5 or larger, only two needed a loan, and just one needed a large loan.

Similar patterns appear for 1980–1987. Nineteen of the 22 states with initial multiples below 0.5 borrowed, and eight needed large loans. Only two states with multiples initially above 1.0 borrowed, and just one needed a large loan. Thus, states with low initial multiples borrowed the most.

Of course, because so many states had low and negative net reserves at the end of 1979, the scale of borrowing during 1980–1987 was much larger than during 1974–1979. Loans during 1974–1979 were $5.5 billion, or 0.94 percent of U.S. total wages in 1975, compared with $24.2 billion during 1980–1987, or 1.77 percent of U.S. total wages in 1984.

Relative to 1974–1979 and 1980–1997, borrowing during 1990–1995 was small. The seven states that needed loans borrowed only $4.8 billion, or 0.22 percent of U.S. total wages in 1991. Note, however, that borrowing was again concentrated in states with low initial RRMs. The loan probabilities in the two lowest intervals during 1990–1995 were 0.44 in the 0.0–0.49 interval (4 of 9) and 0.14 in the 0.5–0.99 interval (3 of 22).

A vertical scan down the borrowing data of Table 1-1 shows a clear pattern of decreasing loan probabilities within a given RRM interval. For states falling in the 0.5–0.99 interval, the probability of borrowing was 0.86 during 1974–1979 (12 of 14), 0.59 during 1980–1987 (10 of 17), and 0.14 during 1990–1995 (3 of 22). Another obvious pattern is the monotonic relationship in grouped data between the initial RRM and the probability of needing a UI loan. States can reduce the risk of recession-related borrowing when they have higher initial reserve ratio multiples.

For additional insight into the lack of state borrowing during the 1990–1992 recession, Table 1-2 provides comparisons of the increases in unemployment rates during recessions. It focuses on state-level ratios of three-year unemployment rates and it also gives the national medians and averages of three-year ratios. The main point is that state-level increases in total unemployment rates (or TURs, as measured in the Current Population Survey [CPS], the monthly household labor force survey)[9] were unusually small during 1990–1992. Nineteen states actually had lower average TURs during 1990–1992 than during 1987–1989, that is, ratios below 1.00. The ratios exceeded 1.25 in just 16 states during 1990–1992, compared with 36, 32, and 37 states, respectively, in the three earlier recessions. The concentration of states with low increases (and even reductions) in unemployment rates during 1990–1992, relative to 1987–1989, underlies the low aggregate unemployment ratio in Table 1-2.

A similar pattern appears in Table 1-3 when the changes in reserve ratio multiples are compared across the four recessions. Relative to the decreases in state-level multiples during 1990–1992, the decreases during the preceding three recessions were two to three times larger. The national ratios decreased by 0.65 during 1969–1973, by 0.98 during 1973–1976, and by 0.62 during 1979–1983, but by only 0.33 during 1989–1992. During the four periods, the number of states in which the decreases exceeded 0.75 were 21, 34, 16, and just 1, respectively. Both Tables 1-2 and 1-3 clearly show that 1990–1992 was a much milder recession than its three immediate predecessors. This must be kept in mind in explaining why state UI trust fund borrowing was so infrequent and on such a small scale during the 1990s.

TRUST FUND DEVELOPMENTS IN THE 1990s

Table 1-4 provides additional detail on individual state trust fund developments during the 1990s, giving the net reserves and RRMs at the end of 1989, 1992, and 1996. Trust fund levels and changes for these years span the most recent episodes of recession and recovery. To characterize the changes in state-level unemployment, the average unemployment rates for 1990–1992 and 1987–1989 are shown as a

Table 1-3 Changes in Reserve Ratio Multiples during Recent Recessions[a]

Year-end change	Increase	Change in RRM (number of states)						State median change	Mean U.S. change
		0.00 to −0.249	−0.25 to −0.499	−0.50 to −0.749	−0.75 to −0.999	−1.00 to 1.499	−1.50 or more		
1969 to 1973	1	4	12	13	9	10	2	−0.66	−0.65
1973 to 1976	1	4	2	10	12	13	9	−0.92	−0.98
1979 to 1983	11	5	10	9	3	10	3	−0.49	−0.62
1989 to 1992	13	20	9	8	1	0	0	−0.20	−0.33

SOURCE: Calculations performed at the Urban Institute using data from the U.S. Department of Labor.
[a] Calculations are shown for the 50 states plus the District of Columbia.

Table 1-4 Net Reserves and Reserve Ratio Multiples by State, December 1989 to December 1996

| State[a] | Net Reserves, Dec. 31 ($mill) | | | Reserve Ratio Multiples | | | | | Ratio of unemployment rates, 1990–92/ 1987–89 |
| | | | | Levels | | | Changes | | |
	1989	1992	1996	1989	1992	1996	1989–92	1992–96	
Connecticut[b]	274	−653	278	0.22	−0.50	0.18	−0.72	0.68	1.947
Maine[c]	206	35	112	0.94	0.15	0.42	−0.78	0.27	1.632
Massachusetts[b]	909	−380	915	0.45	−0.18	0.35	−0.63	0.53	2.236
New Hampshire	204	130	268	0.89	0.55	0.89	−0.34	0.34	2.400
Rhode Island	304	104	116	0.92	0.32	0.31	−0.60	−0.01	2.227
Vermont	197	181	218	1.63	1.41	1.41	−0.21	−0.00	1.783
New Jersey	2,795	2,440	2,029	1.06	0.85	0.60	−0.21	−0.25	1.664
New York[c]	3,181	214	470	0.76	0.05	0.09	−0.71	0.04	1.476
Pennsylvania	1,616	808	2,032	0.55	0.25	0.53	−0.30	0.28	1.297
Puerto Rico	564	749	596	1.82	2.05	1.33	0.24	−0.72	NA[d]
Virgin Islands	28	47	42	2.67	3.21	2.45	0.54	−0.76	NA
Illinois	1,268	848	1,639	0.47	0.28	0.44	−0.19	0.16	1.035
Indiana	770	942	1,273	1.04	1.11	1.19	0.07	0.08	1.083
Michigan[c]	370	−72	1,831	0.13	−0.02	0.45	−0.15	0.47	1.116
Ohio	778	602	1,751	0.30	0.21	0.49	−0.09	0.28	1.037

	1041	1195	1557	0.96	0.93	0.96	-0.03	0.03	1.007
Wisconsin									
Iowa	518	615	719	1.20	1.20	1.11	0.00	-0.09	0.943
Kansas	472	606	651	1.35	1.47	1.26	0.12	-0.21	0.943
Minnesota	359	224	513	0.52	0.27	0.48	-0.24	0.21	1.093
Missouri[c]	372	3	308	0.50	0.00	0.30	-0.50	0.30	1.028
Nebraska	127	161	195	0.89	0.94	0.87	0.05	-0.07	0.671
North Dakota	45	50	50	0.70	0.65	0.49	-0.05	-0.16	0.909
South Dakota	45	50	50	1.46	1.26	0.92	-0.20	-0.34	0.811
Delaware	207	219	258	1.24	1.18	1.10	-0.06	-0.08	1.685
Dist. of Columbia[c]	76	-19	99	0.40	-0.09	0.41	-0.50	0.50	1.405
Florida	2,041	1,444	1,948	1.29	0.79	0.82	-0.50	0.03	1.345
Georgia	1,018	966	1,634	0.96	0.79	0.99	-0.18	0.20	1.032
Maryland	598	146	691	0.75	0.17	0.67	-0.58	0.50	1.387
North Carolina	1,471	1,387	1,336	1.26	1.03	0.75	-0.23	-0.28	1.362
South Carolina	415	433	603	0.66	0.60	0.65	-0.06	0.05	1.154
Virginia	718	507	897	1.17	0.74	1.03	-0.43	0.29	1.366
West Virginia	146	141	157	0.41	0.35	0.33	-0.06	-0.02	1.019
Alabama	623	550	483	1.21	0.90	0.64	-0.31	-0.26	0.965
Kentucky	393	364	501	0.69	0.54	0.58	-0.15	0.04	0.877
Mississippi	388	345	553	1.67	1.26	1.55	-0.42	0.29	0.916

(continued)

Table 1-4 (continued)

| State[a] | Net Reserves, Dec. 31 ($mill) | | | Reserve Ratio Multiples | | | | | Ratio of unemployment rates, 1990–92/ 1987–89 |
| | | | | Levels | | | Changes | | |
	1989	1992	1996	1989	1992	1996	1989–92	1992–96	
Tennessee	657	603	827	0.90	0.69	0.72	-0.21	0.03	1.041
Arkansas	131	81	203	0.40	0.20	0.40	-0.20	0.20	0.934
Louisiana	306	601	1131	0.43	0.72	1.09	0.29	0.37	0.693
Oklahoma	323	419	564	1.34	1.53	1.71	0.19	0.18	0.910
Texas	989	586	642	0.73	0.36	0.30	-0.37	-0.06	0.902
Arizona	493	372	627	0.84	0.55	0.63	-0.29	0.08	1.037
Colorado	239	339	511	0.75	0.87	0.94	0.12	0.07	0.796
Idaho	220	240	266	1.37	1.16	0.94	-0.21	-0.22	0.967
Montana	80	96	126	0.63	0.62	0.67	-0.01	0.05	0.970
Nevada	321	234	348	1.12	0.65	0.64	-0.47	-0.01	1.047
New Mexico	174	239	386	1.48	1.69	2.06	0.21	0.37	0.857
Utah	239	342	524	1.25	1.40	1.46	0.15	0.06	0.885
Wyoming	54	110	147	0.71	1.23	1.39	0.52	0.16	0.756
Alaska	180	232	194	0.93	1.06	0.78	0.12	-0.28	1.005
California	5,419	2,787	2,877	0.92	0.43	0.38	-0.48	-0.05	1.380

Hawaii	340	362	211	1.75	1.68	0.95	-0.07	-0.73	1.058
Oregon	804	1055	941	1.35	1.47	0.94	0.12	-0.53	1.070
Washington	1,364	1,766	1,333	1.07	1.09	0.66	0.02	-0.43	0.937
U.S.Total	36,871	25,847	38,632	0.87	0.54	0.64	-0.33	0.10	1.156

SOURCE: Data are from the UI Service of the U.S. Department of Labor.

[a] Alphabetically within Census division.

[b] States needing large U.S. Treasury loans during 1990–1995.

[c] States needing small U.S. Treasury loans during 1990–1995.

[d] NA = data not available.

ratio. States are arrayed by census division and then alphabetically within each of the nine census divisions. Table 1-4 also identifies the seven states needing UI trust fund loans during 1991–1995.

Four aspects of these data are noteworthy. First, state-level changes in unemployment varied widely during the 1990–1992 downturn. While the national average unemployment rate ratio was 1.156, the state-level ratios ranged from 2.400 (New Hampshire) to 0.671 (Nebraska). Second, the highest unemployment rate ratios were found in states on the Atlantic coast and in California. The New England and Mid Atlantic states had especially large increases in their unemployment rates; arranging the states geographically helps to emphasize this point. Third, the decreases in reserves and reserve ratio multiples were disproportionately large in the states with the largest increases in unemployment. Of the nine states where multiples decreased by 0.50 or more between 1989 and 1992, eight had unemployment rate ratios of 1.345 or higher.[10] Fourth, RRMs decreased in 22 states between the end of 1992 and 1996, a period when trust fund building would have been expected. If we take the RRM as a gauge of trust fund adequacy, the position of those 22 states deteriorated.

The slow pace of reserve accumulation during 1993–1996 is noteworthy and deserves emphasis. One way is to highlight developments in the 10 largest states, which accounted for 52 percent of taxable covered employment and 56 percent of covered payrolls in 1996.[11] Five of the 10 had smaller reserve balances at the end of 1996 than at the end of 1989, and eight had smaller reserve ratio multiples.[12] Weighted by 1996 payrolls, the average RRM for the 10 dropped from 0.72 at the end of 1989 to 0.32 at the end of 1992 and then recovered to 0.41 at the end of 1996. Compared with the national average RRM, their average was 0.15 lower in 1989 (0.72 compared to 0.87) and 0.23 lower in 1996 (0.41 compared to 0.64). In 1996, only three of the 10 largest states had multiples that exceeded 0.50, while four had multiples below 0.40.[13] These states were much more vulnerable to the risk of recession-related financing problems at the start of 1997 than they had been in 1990.

A second way to highlight the slow pace of reserve accumulation during 1992–1996 is to ask the following question: How long would it take to restore reserves to their 1989 level? Between 1992 and 1996, the national reserve ratio multiple increased by only 0.10 (from 0.54 to

0.64), or by an average of 0.025 per year.   At that pace of accumulation, more than eight years would be required to achieve a national multiple of 0.87 (the 1989 RRM).   This would imply an economic recovery lasting more than 12 years, or longer than any expansion since the establishment of UI in the mid 1930s.

Given the strong pace of economic expansion during 1993–1996, a substantial accumulation of reserves would have been anticipated. Annual benefit payouts during 1993–1996 averaged $3.8 billion less than during 1991–1992.   Also, aggregate tax receipts increased substantially; the three-year average for 1994–1996 of $21.8 billion was 42 percent higher than the 1989–1991 average of $15.4 billion.[14]

What distinguishes the UI tax increases during the most recent period of recovery is their comparatively modest size.   The analogous increases following the downturns of 1974–1975 and 1980–1982 exceeded 100 percent and 60 percent, respectively.   Based on earlier recessions, higher UI taxes would have been expected during 1994–1996.

While a detailed analysis of recent changes in UI tax laws lies beyond the scope of this book, there have been UI tax reductions which clearly slowed the pace of trust fund accumulations during 1993–1996. Kansas and North Carolina were especially aggressive in lowering UI taxes, but tax reductions have been widespread during the 1990s.

The slow pace of trust fund accumulations during 1993–1996 has obvious implications for state UI solvency.   In particular, it implies that at the start of 1997, states were more vulnerable to the threat of financing problems than they were seven years earlier, i.e., before the onset of the 1990–1992 recession.

To examine risks of insolvency, a series of simulations was undertaken (details are provided in Appendix A). The simulations used the relationship between decreases in state reserve ratio multiples and increases in average unemployment rates that prevailed during the 1990–1992 recession. Historic patterns of increased state unemployment rates were then fed into this relationship to provide projections of trust fund drawdowns for recessions of differing severity.

Two conclusions emerged from the simulation analysis.

1.   The absence of widespread financing problems during 1990–1992 is attributable to both the mild nature of the recession and

to the comparatively large initial trust state fund balances. The states may not be as lucky in the next recession, for unemployment may be of greater magnitude.

2.   More states needed loans when they entered recessions with their 1996 year-end reserve balances than when they entered with their 1989 reserve balances.

Based on 1993–1996 rates of trust fund accumulation, several states will start the next recession with smaller balances than at the end of 1989. Other things being equal, the smaller balances caused by the slow pace of accumulations during 1993–1996 will cause increased borrowing during the next recession.

In conclusion, it is almost certain that states will enter the next recession with lower trust fund reserves (reserves as a percentage of payroll) than they had before the recession that began in December 1989. To the extent that tax increases and benefit reductions would occur rapidly and in large amounts in a future recession, flexible financing would lessen the need to maintain large reserves before a recession. Chapter 2 examines flexible financing.

Notes

1. The most common arrangement bases weekly benefits on earnings during the highest quarter of the base period, but the weekly benefit is limited to a range defined by a minimum and maximum. A recipient's total potential entitlement typically reflects his or her earnings during the entire one-year base period, for example, one-third of base-period earnings. The potential duration is then the ratio of the potential entitlement to the weekly benefit. The details of monetary eligibility provisions vary widely from state to state.
2. Of the 20 programs in which the taxable wage base exceeded $10,000 in 1996, 18 had indexed tax bases. The other two were Connecticut and Massachusetts.
3. For a recent analysis of experience-rating, particularly on its effects on employer-initiated worker turnover and inter-industry cross subsidies, see Vroman (1996).
4. See Advisory Council on Unemployment Compensation (1995), Chapters 2 and 5 and Appendix E.
5. These are recommendations 2 through 6 in Chapter 2 of the ACUC report. Several of the ACUC recommendations on financial incentives that would encourage states to build large trust fund reserves can be found in Vroman (1990).
6. See, for example, the testimony of Ward (1987), director of the Illinois Department of Employment Security, before the Committee on Ways and Means of the U.S. House of Representatives in December 1987. Her testimony stresses both

the automatic financing features in Illinois' 1987 UI law and the need for each state to determine the level of reserves appropriate to its circumstances.

7. See Miller, Pavosevich, and Vroman (1997), Table 9.3, for a summary of annual debt repayment patterns from 1972 to 1994.

8. Legislation of the early 1980s in the states with largest debts almost always included both benefit reductions and tax increases. See Vroman (1986), Chapter 2.

9. The CPS estimates for small states are incomplete before 1976. Estimates made at the Urban Institute have been used where CPS data were not available.

10. Missouri, the ninth state, had a ratio of only 1.028. The simple correlation between the unemployment rate ratios of Table 1-4 and the 1989–1992 change in state reserve ratio multiples was –0.627. The correlation was much higher (–0.907) when states were weighted by the size of their labor forces.

11. The 10, ranked in descending order according to 1996 payrolls, are California, New York, Texas, Illinois, Florida, Ohio, Pennsylvania, Michigan, New Jersey, and Massachusetts.

12. Note in Table 1-4 that only Ohio and Michigan had higher reserve ratio multiples at the end of 1996 than at the end of 1989.

13. Note California, New York, Texas, and Massachusetts in Table 1-4.

14. Annual data on aggregate UI benefits and employer taxes from 1938 through 1996 appear in columns (10) and (8), respectively, of U.S. Department of Labor ET Handbook 394 (1995) and in later updates to that handbook.

2 Flexible Financing

Because benefit payouts can change sharply from one year to the next, UI programs must be prepared to finance potentially large drawdowns of reserves. Annual benefit payouts can more than double from one year to the next, and high payouts can persist for several years. Individual states have adopted different strategies for addressing these uncertainties. Chapter 1 drew a major distinction between advance (or forward) funding and pay-as-you-go funding. To the extent that pay-as-you-go implies a smaller fund balance prior to recessions, it also implies a higher risk of borrowing during recessions and a greater need for a strong revenue response to offset the effects of recession-related increases in benefit payouts.

This chapter examines flexible financing. Its main concern is with how the UI tax system responds to trust fund drawdowns; it does not attempt to define all aspects of flexible financing. There are three possible parts to a flexible financing strategy. First, and most important, is the response of UI taxes to trust fund drawdowns. This includes both the response caused by experience-rating and that caused by solvency taxes that are automatically triggered when the state's trust fund falls below a designated threshold. The tax response can include the automatic triggering of employee taxes and/or changes in the taxable wage base; it can also include changes in employer taxes. Second, when the trust fund is depleted, the state might restrict benefit payouts, e.g., freeze the maximum weekly benefit. Third, motivated by the trust fund drawdown, a state might respond with legislation that includes both tax increases and benefit reductions. While the magnitude of a legislative response could be measured after the fact, it cannot be forecast and receives only limited attention in this chapter. All three responses act to reduce the size of the trust fund drawdown during a recession.

Flexible financing is a broader concept than tax responsiveness. However, most of this chapter's analysis focuses on tax responsiveness within its cyclical context. Tax-base indexation, a related topic, is studied in Chapter 3. The cyclical responsiveness of UI taxes includes both the speed and the magnitude of the response. Each receives attention in this chapter.

Ultimately, how UI taxes respond to a trust fund drawdown depends on the state's taxation capacity. This capacity, in turn, depends on the taxable share of covered wages (the taxable wage proportion, TWP) and the maximum effective tax rate for the maximum experience-rated tax rate schedule plus the state's solvency taxes. That product, UI taxes as a percentage of covered wages, is the maximum annual rate of inflow that can occur under the given tax statutes. For more than a decade, tax capacity has been decreasing in several states as a direct consequence of state-level downtrends in the TWP, trends that reflect slow adjustments of the tax base over time. In several large states, the tax base has remained at $7,000 per worker since 1983 and tax capacity has been on a downward trend since 1985. This chapter also examines tax capacity.

Since the early 1980s, when the cost of borrowing from the U.S. Treasury increased, states have assumed a larger role in ensuring trust fund solvency. Having adequate taxation capacity is important for ensuring solvency. This chapter traces changes in state-level UI taxes and draws inferences about the evolution of UI taxation during this time of increased state responsibility.

This chapter is divided into four sections: 1) experience-rated taxes, 2) solvency taxes and other solvency measures, 3) the literature on tax responsiveness, and 4) a summary of the findings and policy implications. The analysis in the first two sections focuses heavily on the statutes and on how these have changed over the past 30 years. The analysis is useful for documenting what changes have occurred, but it does not assess their importance. The general conclusion from the empirical studies is that the quantitative importance of flexible financing is rather small. During a serious downturn, flexible financing would not be strong enough to prevent a need for large-scale borrowing to pay UI benefits.

EXPERIENCE-RATING STATUTES

Experience-rating is often quite complicated, and mastering all its nuances requires extensive study. This section focuses on a few key elements of state-level experience-rating, elements that can be traced in readily available publications.[1]

The four experience-rating features selected for emphasis here are not exhaustive, but all are important in answering questions about flexible financing and tax responsiveness.[2] The four are 1) the computation lag, 2) the range of tax rates in state tax rate schedules, 3) the maximum tax rate schedule, and 4) tax capacity. If state systems were evolving towards increased tax responsiveness, one would expect to observe certain patterns of change.

The Computation Lag

To set tax rates for the coming tax year, a UI program examines the overall status of a state's trust fund and also uses the experience indicators for all rateable employers (those with enough years in operation to qualify for experience-rating). The level of the trust fund determines the tax schedule to be used. The date for making this determination is called the "computation date." For nearly all states, the computation date is either June 30th or July 1st. New rates typically become effective on January 1st of the next year, but a few states change tax schedules on July 1st rather than January 1st.

Employers accrue UI tax obligations on a quarterly basis, and tax payments are due one month after the end of each quarter. Except in Massachusetts, payments for the first quarter are due on April 30th.[3] Employers must, therefore, be notified by the end of the first quarter if they are to withhold the appropriate amount from their first-quarter covered payrolls.

If June 30th is the computation date and January 1st is the new tax date, 10 months elapse between the date that the tax schedule is set (June 30th) and the date that the first payments for the next year are received (April 30th). A recession could begin or could become considerably worse during those 10 months, leading to a reduced trust fund balance and making the slated tax schedule and individual employer experience-ratings less appropriate than on the preceding June 30th. Ten additional months of benefit charging would occur, including the first four months of the new year, months in which seasonal benefits are highest.

States are aware of this situation. One possible response would be to move the computation date back six months, to December 31st. That would shorten the lag from 10 to 4 months and would still leave a state the time to determine the necessary tax rates. Increased state interest in flexible financing would, therefore, be expected to shorten the computation lag.

Table 2-1 summarizes computation lags from 1966 to 1996. It includes data for 1975 and 1986 (just before the period of large-scale debt and borrowing of the mid 1970s and after most of the borrowing of the early 1980s). The lags shown in Table 2-1 do not reflect the four-month lag between the start of quarterly accruals and actual quarterly tax payments. Thus, a June 30th computation date, coupled with a January 1st effective date for the new tax schedule, appears in Table 2-1 as a six-month lag.

Table 2-1 shows remarkable stability in the distribution of computation lags. For every year, almost all programs had lags of zero, three, or six months, with about two-thirds of the states having a six-month lag. Interestingly, there were more states with a zero lag in 1966 (10 states) than in 1996 (6 states). There is no evidence that any state has shortened its computation lag. On the contrary, note that the average lag was slightly longer in 1996 than it was in 1986, 1975, or 1966.

New schedules usually become effective on January 1st. Forty-three programs out of 51 used January 1st in 1966, while 48 of 53 used January 1st in 1996. Two fewer states used July 1st as the start date for the new tax year in 1996 than did in to 1966. Nothing in the data suggests that states have acted to reduce the lag between the computation date and the date when new tax schedules take effect.

The Structure of Tax Rates: Minimums, Maximums, and Ranges

States can more effectively assign benefit charges to individual employers when operative tax rates span a wider range of potential rates. Having a wider range of rates within individual tax schedules also adds to tax responsiveness, for it is then easier to raise employer rates in response to less favorable individual experience indicators.[4] A wider range of rates moves a state's tax system towards increased tax responsiveness.[5]

Table 2-1 Computation Lags and New Tax Schedule Dates, 1966 to 1996[a]

Year	Length of computation lag (number of UI programs)					Average lag (months)	Date new tax schedules take effect			Total programs
	0 months	3 months	6 months	Other	Total programs		Jan. 1	April 1	July 1	
1966	10	7	33	1	51	4.4	43	1	7	51
1975	8	7	35	1	51	4.6	44	1	6	51
1986	8	7	33	4	52	4.5	47	0	5	52
1996	6	7	37	3	53	4.8	49	0	4	53

SOURCE: U.S. Department of Labor, 1966 and 1975; National Foundation for Unemployment Compensation and Workers' Compensation, 1986 and 1996.

[a] The counts show the number of UI programs with the indicated features in each year. Puerto Rico and the Virgin Islands are not included in 1966 and 1975. Puerto Rico is not included in 1986.

Because state UI programs operate within a federal-state statutory framework, several aspects of UI taxes levied by the states must conform with federal requirements. The Tax Equity and Fiscal Responsibility Act of 1983, or TEFRA (Public Law 97-248), contained several provisions for financing UI. What is most important for the discussion here is that the maximum FUT credit offset was increased from 2.7 percent to 5.4 percent effective January 1, 1985. Thus, from that date, to have a federally approved experience-rating system, a state UI program had to have a maximum experience-rated tax rate of at least 5.4 percent.

To put the effects of TEFRA into perspective, Tables 2-2, 2-3, and 2-4 give tax rate information for 1966 to 1996, showing the distributions of minimum tax rates, maximum tax rates, and the range of rates on January 1st. The data in these tables reflect the actual tax rate schedules in effect in the indicated years. Three-year intervals are shown for 1966 to 1978 and two-year intervals thereafter. Because of the change mandated by TEFRA, tax rates are given for 1984, 1985, and 1986.

As background to the discussion, keep in mind that UI trust funds had major drawdowns during 1975–1977 and again during 1980–1983. Net reserves also decreased during 1990–1992 but by much smaller relative amounts. The years 1962–1969 and 1984–1989 saw large increases in trust fund balances.[6]

The tax rate distribution remained stable between 1966 and 1972. The average minimum tax rate was 0.4 to 0.6 percent, while the average maximum rate was 3.5 to 3.6 percent, and the average range of rates was about 3.0 percent. About three-quarters of the programs had a range of tax rates between 2.1 and 4.0 percent.

From 1972 to 1984, the distribution of minimum rates, maximum rates, and ranges increased markedly; by 1984, the respective national averages were 1.3 percent, 6.1 percent, and 4.8 percent. These increases reflect responses to the financing problems of the mid 1970s and early 1980s.

The effects of TEFRA on maximum tax rates are obvious in Table 2-3. Twenty states had a maximum rate below 5.4 percent in 1984. In 1985, no state had a maximum rate below 5.4 percent, and the average maximum rate increased from 6.1 percent to 7.0 percent. Further, the average range of tax rates went from 4.8 percent to 6.0 percent (Table 2-4).

Table 2-2 Distribution of Minimum UI Tax Rates, 1966 to 1996 (number of states)[a]

Year	0	0.1 to 0.2%	0.3 to 0.6%	0.7 to 1.0%	1.1 to 1.5%	1.6 to 2.0%	2.1 to 2.5%	2.6% and above	State average (%)
1966	9	12	11	8	8	2	0	2	0.6
1969	12	15	13	7	3	1	0	1	0.4
1972	6	18	10	7	5	3	1	2	0.6
1975	7	11	8	8	8	2	2	6	0.9
1978	3	9	11	4	10	2	3	11	1.2
1980	5	10	9	8	7	6	2	6	1.0
1982	2	12	9	10	7	3	4	6	1.1
1984	1	7	9	10	7	6	7	6	1.3
1985	4	10	8	10	6	6	5	4	1.0
1986	3	11	12	7	7	7	5	1	0.9
1988	4	12	14	7	7	6	2	1	0.8
1990	4	18	17	5	4	4	0	1	0.6
1992	6	15	15	6	4	2	3	2	0.7
1994	7	13	15	7	3	3	5	0	0.6
1996	8	13	16	5	4	3	3	1	0.6

SOURCE: Data from 1966 to 1984 are taken from U.S. Department of Labor, *Significant Provisions of State Unemployment Insurance Laws*, various issues. Data from 1986 to 1996 are taken from National Foundation for Unemployment Compensation and Workers' Compensation, *Highlights of State Unemployment Compensation Laws*, various issues.

[a] State averages are the unweighted averages for 52 or 53 programs, i.e., they include the Virgin Islands from 1978 onward.

Table 2-3 Distribution of Maximum UI Tax Rates, 1966 to 1996 (number of states)[a]

Year	2.7%	2.8 to 4.0%	4.1 to 5.3%	5.4%	5.5 to 6.4%	6.5 to 7.4%	7.5 to 9.0%	9.1% and above	State average (%)
1966	18	23	10	0	0	1	0	0	3.5
1969	15	27	8	0	1	1	0	0	3.5
1972	11	27	13	0	0	1	0	0	3.6
1975	8	25	16	0	2	1	0	0	3.9
1978	5	21	16	1	6	2	2	0	4.4
1980	2	19	13	1	12	4	2	0	4.8
1982	0	16	15	2	8	6	5	1	5.2
1984	0	7	13	3	9	9	8	4	6.1
1985	0	0	0	15	9	11	13	5	7.0
1986	0	0	0	17	8	8	12	8	7.1
1988	0	0	0	18	9	5	12	9	7.0
1990	0	0	0	22	9	7	9	6	6.7
1992	0	0	0	21	7	9	10	6	6.8
1994	0	0	0	18	8	7	15	5	7.0
1996	0	0	0	16	11	6	17	3	6.9

SOURCE: Data from 1966 to 1984 are taken from U.S. Department of Labor, *Significant Provisions of State Unemployment Insurance Laws*, various issues. Data from 1986 to 1996 are taken from National Foundation for Unemployment Compensation and Workers' Compensation, *Highlights of State Unemployment Compensation Laws*, various issues.

[a] State averages are the unweighted averages for 52 or 53 programs, i.e., they include the Virgin Islands from 1978 onward.

Table 2-4 Distribution of the Range of UI Tax Rates, 1966 to 1996 (number of states)[a]

Year	0	0.1 to 2.0%	2.1 to 3.0%	3.1 to 4.0%	4.1 to 5.0%	5.1 to 6.0%	6.1 to 8.0%	8.1% and above	State average (%)
1966	1	6	26	14	3	2	0	0	2.9
1969	0	5	26	16	3	2	0	0	3.1
1972	1	5	22	19	4	1	0	0	3.0
1975	2	9	17	17	6	1	0	0	2.9
1978	5	5	14	17	5	4	3	0	3.2
1980	3	2	12	15	11	6	4	0	3.8
1982	3	4	7	13	12	5	8	1	4.1
1984	4	1	4	15	6	6	15	2	4.8
1985	0	0	2	5	11	11	14	10	6.0
1986	0	0	2	2	11	12	17	9	6.2
1988	0	0	1	4	7	16	14	11	6.2
1990	0	0	1	2	10	18	11	11	6.2
1992	0	0	1	1	12	16	13	10	6.1
1994	0	0	0	0	10	20	11	12	6.3
1996	0	0	0	0	10	20	15	8	6.3

SOURCE: Data from 1966 to 1984 are taken from U.S. Department of Labor, *Significant Provisions of State Unemployment Insurance Laws*, various issues. Data from 1986 to 1996 are taken from National Foundation for Unemployment Compensation and Workers' Compensation, *Highlights of State Unemployment Compensation Laws*, various issues.

[a] State averages are the unweighted averages for 52 or 53 programs, i.e., they include the Virgin Islands from 1978 onward.

Since 1985, the structure of UI tax rates has been very stable. The average maximum rate has been between 6.7 percent and 7.1 percent in all subsequent years (Table 2-3). Minimum rates declined somewhat after 1985, and the range of rates has remained stable. Beginning with 1985, the average range was between 6.0 percent and 6.3 percent. After TEFRA came into effect, the range of state-level tax rates has been consistently about twice that for 1966–1972. Compared to 25 or 30 years ago, there is now a much wider range of rates over which experience-rating can operate. All states had a range of tax rates of at least 4.1 percent in 1996, and eight had ranges that exceeded 8.0 percent. TEFRA has clearly improved the effectiveness with which state experience-rating systems rate individual employers. This increased effectiveness in assigning appropriate rates also implies an increased ability for average tax rates (on taxable payrolls) to respond to trust fund drawdowns.

Two added points about the tax rate distributions should be noted. First, there is always a concentration of states at the minimum acceptable maximum tax rate, which has been 5.4 percent since 1985 (Table 2-3). However, only about half of all state maximums have been in the range of 5.4 to 6.4 percent in recent years. States vary in how they set maximum rates.[7]   Second, there was only a modest increase in maximum rates after the 1990–1992 recession. The average maximum increased from 6.7 percent in 1990 to 7.0 percent in 1994 and then decreased to 6.9 percent in 1996.

The increases in the maximum tax rates and in the range of tax rates after 1984 increase the UI financing system's cyclical responsiveness to trust fund drawdowns. Quite simply, a wider range of higher tax rates can be imposed as state trust fund balances decline and individual employer-experience measures deteriorate. This increases the cyclical variability of the average tax rate on taxable payrolls.

Maximum Tax Rate Schedules and Tax Capacity

The tax rate distributions summarized in Tables 2-2, 2-3, and 2-4 are for the tax schedules used between 1966 and 1996. In many states, UI tax statutes provide for several tax rate schedules. The schedule for a given year is based on the statewide trust fund balance on the computation date; successively lower balances trigger successively higher tax rate schedules. In other words, the experience-rating mechanism that sets individual employer tax rates uses both the statewide fund balance (to select the appropriate tax schedule) and each employer's experience (reserve ratio or benefit ratio, depending on the state's experience-rating system[8]) to set tax rates for individual employers.

To get an idea of UI taxes that could potentially be collected, one must examine the top tax rate schedules and their tax rates. Movement to the top schedule would increase a state's tax revenues. Taxation at the top schedule, in conjunction with the taxable wage proportion (the TWP, or taxable wages as a fraction of total covered wages), shows the maximum potential revenues that could be collected through a state's experience-rating mechanism. Thus, there is interest in the top tax schedules both to show UI tax responsiveness and to assess tax capacity for a state.

A UI program's ability to raise revenues depends on both experience-rated taxes and solvency taxes. A complete assessment of tax responsiveness and tax capacity would consider both types of taxes. The following discussion focuses on experience-rated taxes.

It should also be noted that multiple tax rate schedules, although contemplated in UI tax statutes, are not always used in practice. Massachusetts, in the 1990s, provides a vivid example. The current set of eight tax rate schedules was to have come into effect in 1992. For each of the five years from 1992 to 1996, however, the schedule used was lower than the one indicated in the tax statute. Massachusetts enacted special legislation to override the statute. The following analysis assumes, however, that maximum tax rate schedules actually would be imposed if fund balances were depleted to the point where the trigger mechanism called for the top schedule.

Table 2-5 shows the maximum tax rates for the top experience-rating schedules and the factors that determine tax capacity for 1986 and 1996. Tax capacity (potential tax revenue as a percentage of total wages) reflects both the TWP and the average tax rate when taxes are levied according to the top schedule. The average rate depends on the tax rates in the top schedule and on the distribution of employers (and their taxable wages) across individual rate categories. The average rates shown in Table 2-5 are simple averages of the minimum and the maximum for the top tax rate schedule.

Table 2-5 Tax Capacity for the Top Experience-Rated Tax Schedules, 1986 and 1996

State	1986				1996				Tax capacity	
	TWP	Max. tax rate (%)	Avg. tax rate (%)	Tax capacity	TWP	Max. tax rate (%)	Avg. tax rate (%)	Tax capacity	Change	% change
Alabama	0.460	5.4	2.95	1.36	0.352	6.8	3.73	1.31	-0.05	-3.4
Alaska[a]	0.681	6.5	3.75	2.55	0.654	6.5	3.75	2.45	-0.10	-4.0
Arizona	0.405	5.4	4.15	1.68	0.316	5.4	4.15	1.31	-0.37	-22.0
Arkansas	0.477	6.0	3.05	1.45	0.426	6.0	3.05	1.30	-0.16	-10.7
California	0.353	5.4	3.35	1.18	0.250	5.4	3.35	0.84	-0.35	-29.2
Colorado	0.415	5.4	3.05	1.27	0.383	5.4	2.75	1.05	-0.21	-16.8
Connecticut	0.324	6.4	3.95	1.28	0.305	6.9	4.45	1.36	0.08	6.1
Delaware	0.402	7.0	3.55	1.43	0.300	8.0	4.05	1.22	-0.21	-14.9
District of Columbia	0.351	5.4	3.10	1.09	0.267	7.4	4.65	1.24	0.15	14.1
Florida	0.428	5.4	2.75	1.18	0.319	5.4	2.75	0.88	-0.30	-25.5
Georgia	0.412	5.7	3.21	1.32	0.331	8.1	4.08	1.35	0.03	2.3
Hawaii[a]	0.686	5.4	4.00	2.74	0.711	5.4	3.90	2.77	0.03	1.1
Idaho[a]	0.693	6.8	4.85	3.36	0.673	6.8	4.85	3.26	-0.10	-2.9
Illinois	0.378	6.6	3.40	1.29	0.303	6.6	3.40	1.03	-0.26	-19.8
Indiana	0.372	5.4	3.35	1.25	0.293	5.7	3.55	1.04	-0.21	-16.5
Iowa[a]	0.582	7.0	3.75	2.18	0.531	9.0	4.50	2.39	0.21	9.5

Kansas	0.483	5.4	2.71	1.31	0.416	6.4	3.20	1.33	0.02	1.6
Kentucky	0.443	10.0	5.50	2.44	0.349	10.0	5.50	1.92	−0.52	−21.2
Louisiana	0.396	6.0	3.15	1.25	0.339	6.0	3.15	1.07	−0.18	−14.4
Maine	0.445	6.5	4.45	1.98	0.330	7.5	4.95	1.63	−0.35	−17.5
Maryland	0.373	6.0	4.40	1.64	0.316	8.9	5.45	1.72	0.08	4.9
Massachusetts	0.385	7.2	5.10	1.96	0.358	9.3	6.35	2.27	0.31	15.8
Michigan	0.394	9.0	4.50	1.77	0.308	9.0	4.65	1.43	−0.34	−19.2
Minnesota[a]	0.471	7.5	4.25	2.00	0.477	9.0	4.80	2.29	0.29	14.4
Mississippi	0.465	6.4	3.25	1.51	0.365	6.4	3.25	1.19	−0.33	−21.5
Missouri	0.406	7.8	3.90	1.58	0.333	7.8	3.90	1.30	−0.28	−18.0
Montana[a]	0.714	6.4	4.05	2.89	0.686	6.4	4.05	2.78	−0.11	−3.9
Nebraska	0.421	5.4	2.75	1.16	0.326	5.4	2.75	0.90	−0.26	−22.6
Nevada[a]	0.590	5.4	3.25	1.92	0.579	5.4	2.83	1.64	−0.28	−14.7
New Hampshire	0.408	6.5	4.65	1.90	0.308	6.5	3.28	1.01	−0.89	−46.8
New Jersey[a]	0.456	6.2	3.70	1.69	0.458	6.9	4.00	1.83	0.14	8.6
New Mexico[a]	0.549	5.4	4.05	2.22	0.541	5.4	4.05	2.19	−0.03	−1.5
New York	0.322	6.4	4.25	1.37	0.213	5.4	3.25	0.69	−0.68	−49.4
North Carolina[a]	0.515	5.7	2.90	1.49	0.455	5.7	2.85	1.30	−0.20	−13.2
North Dakota[a]	0.567	5.0	2.75	1.56	0.548	5.4	2.95	1.62	0.06	3.7
Ohio	0.390	5.4	2.80	1.09	0.334	6.5	3.30	1.10	0.01	0.9

48

Table 2-5 (continued)

State	1986				1996				Tax capacity	
	TWP	Max. tax rate (%)	Avg. tax rate (%)	Tax capacity	TWP	Max. tax rate (%)	Avg. tax rate (%)	Tax capacity	Change	% change
Oklahoma[a]	0.462	6.2	3.35	1.55	0.457	9.2	4.75	2.17	0.62	40.3
Oregon[a]	0.629	5.4	3.80	2.39	0.607	5.4	3.80	2.31	-0.08	-3.5
Pennsylvania	0.402	9.2	5.35	2.15	0.297	9.2	5.35	1.59	-0.56	-26.1
Puerto Rico	0.588	5.4	4.18	2.45	0.466	5.4	3.95	1.84	-0.61	-25.0
Rhode Island[a]	0.554	8.4	5.35	2.96	0.556	8.3	5.20	2.89	-0.07	-2.5
South Carolina	0.436	5.4	3.35	1.46	0.327	5.4	3.32	1.09	-0.37	-25.7
South Dakota	0.465	10.5	6.00	2.79	0.364	9.5	5.50	2.00	-0.79	-28.2
Tennessee	0.414	10.0	5.25	2.17	0.306	10.0	5.25	1.61	-0.57	-26.1
Texas	0.377	6.0	3.05	1.15	0.337	6.0	3.00	1.01	-0.14	-12.1
Utah[a]	0.576	8.0	4.15	2.39	0.575	8.0	4.15	2.39	0.00	-0.2
Vermont	0.469	8.4	4.85	2.27	0.351	8.4	4.85	1.70	-0.57	-25.2
Virginia	0.392	6.2	3.45	1.35	0.315	6.4	3.35	1.06	-0.30	-22.0
Virgin Islands[a]	0.778	9.0	4.55	3.54	0.590	9.0	4.55	2.68	-0.86	-24.2
Washington[a]	0.532	5.4	3.94	2.10	0.584	5.4	3.88	2.27	0.17	8.1
West Virginia	0.423	7.5	4.50	1.90	0.357	7.5	4.50	1.61	-0.30	-15.6
Wisconsin	0.500	6.7	3.35	1.68	0.392	8.9	4.59	1.80	0.12	7.3

Wyoming[a]	0.508	8.5	4.88	2.48	0.485	8.8	4.55	2.21	-0.27	-10.9
National	0.408	6.4	3.72	1.52	0.342	6.8	3.85	1.32	-0.20	-13.3
Indexed states	0.523	6.3	3.75	1.96	0.519	6.8	3.94	2.05	0.09	4.3
Nonindexed states	0.386	6.5	3.72	1.44	0.306	6.8	3.82	1.17	-0.27	-18.5

SOURCE: U.S. Department of Labor, *Comparison of State Unemployment Insurance Laws*.

[a] States with indexed tax bases.

Other things being equal, experience-rated UI taxes will be potentially more responsive to a trust fund drawdown when three elements are greater. First, the response will be greater when the TWP is greater. The TWP declined for most state UI programs (48 of 53) between 1986 and 1996 (Table 2-5). Nationwide, the decline was from 0.408 to 0.342, or 16.2 percent. For 28 states, the TWP not only declined, but its 1996 value was at least 15 percent less than its 1986 value. Note that the average TWP in 1986 for the 18 states with indexed taxable wage bases was practically the same as in 1996 (0.523 versus 0.519),[9] while the average for the other programs declined from 0.386 to 0.306, or by 20.7 percent.

A second element influencing the experience-rated tax response is the maximum tax rate for the top tax schedule. Between 1986 and 1996, the maximum rate increased in 19 UI programs, declined in 3, and remained unchanged in the remaining 31. The average tax rate for the top schedule (the simple average of the minimum and the maximum rates) increased in 18 programs, decreased in 14, and remained unchanged in 21. The average change nationwide was a modest increase of 0.13 percentage points (from 3.72 percent of taxable wages in 1986 to 3.85 percent in 1996), or 3.5 percent. The average percentage change in the top average tax rate was slightly larger for UI programs with indexed tax bases (from 3.75 to 3.94, or 5.2 percent) than for nonindexed programs (3.72 to 3.82, or 2.9 percent). Overall, the average tax rate for the top tax schedule changed little.

The third element in tax responsiveness is the trigger that activates the highest tax rate schedule. If the trigger increases relative to covered wages, the state will move to the highest schedule more quickly when a recession-related drawdown occurs. States vary in how they set the trigger (for example, as an absolute level of the trust fund, as a reserve ratio, or as a reserve ratio multiple). Comparisons of 1986 and 1996 for the 39 programs with triggers expressed as reserve ratio multiples or reserve ratios show higher triggers in 4 programs, lower triggers in 11, and no change in the remaining 24.[10] On average, triggers moved modestly towards a slower response of the top tax schedule.

Given these three elements of experience-rated tax responsiveness, overall responsiveness was smaller in 1996 than in 1986, mainly because taxable wages grew more slowly than covered wages during that period. The decline in the TWP was substantial, over 16 percent nationwide, but the average rate for the top tax schedule increased only slightly, and the average trigger threshold for the top schedule decreased slightly. Individual states had different combinations of these changes. Over half the states showed little or no change in the average rate for the top tax rate schedule or for the trigger for the top rate. Thus, while tax responsiveness cannot be quantified, the trend was towards decreased responsiveness, due to the decline in TWP in so many programs.

Table 2-5 also shows that tax capacity for experience-rated taxes (defined as the TWP times the average tax rate for the top tax rate schedule and expressed as a percentage of covered wages) fell between 1986 and 1996 for most UI programs,[11] primarily due to widespread decreases in the TWP. For nonindexed states, the average TWP decreased from 0.386 in 1986 to 0.306 in 1996. Nationwide, the average rate for the top tax schedule increased, but only modestly.

The two right-hand columns in Table 2-5 focus on changes in tax capacity between 1986 and 1996. The average national decline was 13.3 percent (from 1.52 to 1.32, or 0.20 percentage points). Thirty programs had declines of at least 10.0 percent, while only four had increases of 10.0 percent or more. Between 1986 and 1996, the maximum revenue-generating capacity of the experience-rated portion of the UI tax system fell by about 13 percent.

Another interesting feature of Table 2-5 is the contrast in levels and trends in tax capacity for indexed and nonindexed states. There were 18 indexed programs during the decade covered by the table. Indexed programs had a higher average tax capacity than nonindexed programs in 1986 (1.96 versus 1.44 percent of total wages) and again in 1996 (2.05 versus 1.17 percent). During 1986–1996, indexed programs maintained their tax capacity, but tax capacity fell still further in the nonindexed programs: average tax capacity rose by 4.3 percent in indexed programs but fell by 18.5 percent in nonindexed ones. (Chapter 3 examines indexation in more detail.)

This analysis of the experience-rating statutes in effect from 1966 to 1996 provides four main findings.

1. The lag between the computation date and the date that new tax rates become effective did not change measurably over the past 30 years.

2. During that period, the maximum tax rates and the range of tax rates actually in effect rose substantially. The rise in each stems mainly from the TEFRA requirement that the maximum experience-rated tax rate be at least 5.4 percent as of 1985. Post-1984 increases improved the ability of UI taxes to respond to trust fund drawdowns. However, since 1986, the distribution of both the maximums and the range of rates has been remarkably stable.

3. The share of total taxable wages fell markedly during the past decade, which has reduced both tax responsiveness and tax capacity since 1986.

4. During the past decade, the maximum experience-rated tax rates, the average tax rate on the top tax schedule, and the top tax schedule triggers have not changed much on average. Clearly, while these three elements can limit tax responsiveness, they do not add to it.

Any conclusion about what the four findings mean when taken together must be tentative, but it is likely that the wider range of rates is the most important, and the decline in the TWP is next in importance. The first and fourth points above are likely of minor importance. On balance, when 1986–1996 is compared to earlier periods, it would appear that tax responsiveness has increased. However, between 1986 and 1996, tax responsiveness decreased because the range of rates remained stable while the TWP decreased. Since the TWP did not fall in indexed programs, the increase in their tax responsiveness around 1985 was not eroded between the 1986 and 1996.

There are three findings on the tax capacity of experience-rated taxes for 1986–1996.

1. Average tax capacity fell over the period.

2. That decline was concentrated in states with nonindexed tax bases.

3. The tax capacity of programs having indexed taxable wage bases consistently exceeded that of nonindexed programs.

In 1996, the differential was 0.88 percentage points, or 75 percent (2.05 percent of covered wages versus 1.17 percent). States with indexed programs were much more successful in sustaining their ability to generate tax revenues between 1986 and 1996, a decade in which their economies grew.

SOLVENCY PROVISIONS IN STATE UI LAWS

Several states now have UI statutes with provisions that automatically raise taxes and/or reduce benefits whenever the trust fund balance falls below a certain threshold. These provisions, often called "solvency provisions," operate in addition to experience-rating. In reserve-ratio states, which typically have several tax rate schedules, the solvency tax may be a direct extension of the progression of taxes across the regular tax rate schedules[12] or it may be separate. In benefit-ratio states, solvency taxes often operate apart from experience-rated taxes.

The origins and evolution of solvency provisions vary. Some states created ad hoc arrangements, intended as temporary fixes, when their trust funds were inadequate. Others have made solvency provisions permanent features of their UI statutes. At least two states, Illinois and Pennsylvania, overhauled their tax and benefit statutes in the late 1980s. Both intended to reduce the average trust fund balance over the business cycle and add flexibility. Recession-related drawdowns were to be countered by automatic tax increases and benefit reductions as the fund balance fell past certain thresholds. This section does not examine the motivations of individual states; it simply documents various solvency features.

There is general acknowledgment that states have increased their reliance on solvency taxes and on other provisions for flexible financing, especially since 1980. Several events in the early 1980s may have caused this shift. First, during the back-to-back recessions of 1980–1983, 31 states borrowed from the federal loan account to pay benefits. Second, federal loan policy became significantly tighter. Deferrals of FUTA credit reductions (for loan repayments) were eliminated in 1980,[13] and interest-free loans (except for very short-term loans) were eliminated in 1982. At the time that borrowing became less attractive to states, sentiment grew, strongly voiced by the employer community, that large trust fund balances might not be desirable. That sentiment has also motivated states to make their financing systems more responsive.

Since 1980, many state legislatures, faced with insolvent UI trust fund accounts, moved to make their UI tax and/or benefit flows more responsive during recessions. Four solvency provisions that can make a UI program more responsive are 1) solvency taxes levied on employers, 2) changes in the taxable wage base, 3) employee taxes, and 4) benefit freezes and/or reductions. The common element in all four is a trigger that comes into operation when the trust fund balance falls below a set threshold (or thresholds). Usually, the trigger is both clearly defined in the statute and automatic, but its activation requires a decision in a few states.[14]

Solvency taxes on employers are the most frequent solvency provision, and flexible benefit provisions are the second most frequent. Flexible employee taxes and flexible tax bases are less common. (The flexible tax base, as the term is used in this chapter, refers to a tax base that responds to changes in the trust fund balance. Tax-base indexing, that it, tying the tax base to average wages in the state, is examined in Chapter 3.)

Table 2-6 shows the states that have solvency taxes, the potential range of added tax rates, and the actual rates in effect during 1988 and 1996. The table also shows the first year a state had a solvency provision, and, for a few states, the last year a solvency tax was authorized. Most states with a solvency tax established the tax in the 1980s; of the 36 states listed in Table 2-6, 23 began the tax in the 1980s, 9 in the 1970s, and 3 in the 1990s. States that had a solvency tax before 1980 usually had financing problems during the recessions of the early-to-mid 1970s, e.g., five northeastern states and Michigan.[15] Six states have allowed their solvency tax to lapse.

Solvency taxes on employers were authorized in 31 states in 1988 and in 30 states in 1996. Fourteen states collected revenues from their solvency taxes in 1988 and 1996. Note that the maximum potential solvency tax rate exceeded 1.0 percent of taxable wages for 18 programs in 1988 and for 20 programs in 1996. In both years, about half the states with an active solvency tax levied the tax at a flat rate, while

Table 2-6 Evolution of UI Solvency Taxes

State	First year	Last year	Solvency Taxes in 1988			Solvency Taxes in 1996		
			Present	Range of rates (%)	Rates in 1988 (%)	Present	Range of rates (%)	Rates in 1996 (%)
Alabama	1984	1990	X	0.0–0.7	0.0			
Alaska	1981		X	0.4–1.1	0.26–0.83	X	0.4–1.1	0.0
Arkansas	1975		X	0.1–0.5	0.4	X	–0.1 to 0.8	0.4
California	1985		X	0.2–0.81	0.0	X	0.2–0.81	0.0
Colorado	1990					X	0.0–1.1	0.0
Connecticut	1974		X	0.0–1.0	0.7	X	0.0–1.5	1.5
Delaware	1961		X	1.1–2.5	1.1–1.5	X	0.7–2.5	0.7
District of Columbia	1980	1992	X	0.9	0.0			
Georgia	1985		X	0.0–3.24	0.0–3.24	X	0.0–2.7	0.0–2.7
Hawaii	1977	1991	X	–0.5 to 2.4	0.0			
Illinois	1982		X	0.0–0.6	0.4	X	0.0–0.6	0.4
Louisiana	1983		X	0.0–1.8	0.0	X	0.0–1.8	0.01–0.21
Maine	1993					X	0.4	0.4
Maryland	1989					X	0.1–2.0	0.6
Michigan	1972		X	0.0–2.0	0.0	X	0.0–2.0	0.0
Minnesota	1983		X	0.0–1.2	0.0	X	0.0–1.35	0.0
Mississippi	1985	1994	X	1.0	0.0			
Missouri	1983		X	0.0–1.8	0.0	X	0.0–1.8	0.0–1.8

(continued)

Table 2-6 (continued)

State	First year	Last year	Solvency Taxes in 1988			Solvency Taxes in 1996		
			Present	Range of rates (%)	Rates in 1988 (%)	Present	Range of rates (%)	Rates in 1996 (%)
Nebraska	1996					X	0.0–1.08	0.0
New Hampshire	1976		X	0.5	0.0	X	0.5	0.0
New Jersey	1984		X	0.0–1.6	0.0	X	0.0–0.69	0.0
New York	1973		X	0.–1.0	1.0	X	0.1–1.7	0.7–1.7
North Carolina	1984		X	0.0–1.14	0.0–1.14	X	0.0–1.14	0.0
Ohio	1972		X	0.0–2.55	0.9–2.6	X	0.0–2.55	0.6–2.0
Oklahoma	1984		X	0.0–2.3	0.0	X	0.0–3.07	0.0
Pennsylvania	1979		X	0.5	0.5	X	−0.01 to 1.61	0.07–0.43
Rhode Island	1975		X	0.2–1.95	0.2–1.8	X	0.3	0.0
South Carolina	1985?		X	0.35–1.05	0.0	X	0.35–1.05	0.0
South Dakota	1984		X	0.1–1.5	0.0	X	0.1–1.5	0.0
Tennessee	1984	1989	X	0.0–0.7	0.0			
Texas	1982		X	0.0–2.0	0.63–2.0	X	0.0–2.0	0.18
Virginia	1983		X	0.2	0.0	X	0.2	0.0
Virgin Islands	1985		X	0.5–1.0	0.0	X	0.5–1.0	0.0
West Virginia	1981	1991	X	0.0–3.1	1.0			
Wisconsin	1982		X	0.–1.7	0.0–1.7	X	0.0–0.9	0.0–0.9
Wyoming	1989					X	0.0–1.25	0.0

57

States with solvency taxes	31	30
States with taxes activated	14	14

SOURCE: U.S. Department of Labor, *Comparison of State Unemployment Insurance Laws*, National Foundation for Unemployment Corporation and Workers' Compensation, *Highlights of State Unemployment*, and Commerce Clearing House summaries of UI laws in individual states.

about half used a range of rates. Thus, between 1988 and 1996 there was no trend in the number of states with solvency taxes.

Many states added solvency taxes as part of more comprehensive law reforms dealing with insolvency. Those taxes remain in place and serve to decrease the degree of counter-cyclicality in the UI system. For instance, after having severe solvency problems in the early 1980s, Minnesota raised the trigger for its highest tax schedule in 1988 from $80 million to $200 million, in effect activating the top schedule earlier in the face of a trust fund drawdown. Minnesota also added a solvency tax that can change quarterly, adding 10 percent to scheduled tax rates when the trust fund falls below $150 million and 15 percent (up to 1.35 percentage points for employers at the maximum tax rate) when the fund falls below $75 million. In short, when Minnesota's trust fund balance falls below $75 million, there is a 15 percent add-on to experience-rated tax rates.

Other solvency features are summarized in Table 2-7. Variable employee taxes and flexible tax bases are not common. Only three states (Alaska, New Jersey, and Pennsylvania) had a variable employee tax in 1996[16] and three (the District of Columbia, Louisiana, and Missouri) had trust-fund-activated flexible tax bases. Several others used one of these features in earlier years but have allowed it to lapse.

Flexible benefits are more common. Fourteen states enacted some form of flexible benefits between 1983 and 1996, and 11 were still using them in 1996. All states but Delaware target high-wage claimants. Typically, the maximum weekly benefit amount (the WBA) can be frozen or even reduced if the trust fund drops below a given level or levels. Twelve of the 14 states freeze or reduce benefits. Two vary the wage replacement rate (benefits as a proportion of lost wages), but Pennsylvania does not reduce benefits for low-wage claimants. Minnesota raises the replacement rate when its trust fund is depleted.

In 11 of the 14 states, the benefit trigger is either the absolute level of the state's trust fund or its trust fund balance measured as a ratio to covered wages (in Pennsylvania, as a ratio to benefit payouts). Other elements of the triggers are almost always related to financing variables, for example, employer tax rates (four states) or outstanding Title XII loans (Vermont). The trigger for three states has more than one indicator, with the Illinois trigger having three separate elements.[17]

Table 2-7 UI Flexible Financing Features Other Than Solvency Taxes on Employers

State	Flexible benefit features					Flex. benefit trigger		Flexible employee tax or flexible tax base			
	First year	Last year	Reduce replacement rate	Freeze max. WBA	Reduce max. WBA	Reserve or reserve ratio	All other	First year	Last year	Employee tax	Tax base
Alabama								1938	1990	X	
Alaska								1955		X	
Delaware	1988			X	X			1994	1996		X
District of Columbia						X					
Georgia	1989	1991		X		X					
Hawaii								1988	1991		X
Illinois	1991			X		X	X				
Iowa								1984	1986		X
Kentucky	1987			X		X	X				
Louisiana	1996				X	X		1996			X
Maine	1992			X	X		X				
Minnesota	1983		X[a]			X					
Missouri								1985			X
Montana								1975	1977		X
New Jersey								1938	Note b	X	

(continued)

Table 2-7 (continued)

State	Flexible benefit features First year	Last year	Reduce replace-ment rate	Freeze max. WBA	Reduce max. WBA	Flex. benefit trigger Reserve or reserve ratio	All other	Flexible employee tax or flexible tax base First year	Last year	Employee tax	Tax base
North Carolina	1984	1987		X		X					
North Dakota	1991			X		X	X				
Ohio								1992	1995		X
Oklahoma	1984				X		X				
Pennsylvania	1990		X			X		1990		X	
Vermont	1987			X			X				
Washington	1985	1993		X		X					
West Virginia								1988	1991	X	
Wyoming	1984			X	X	X					
Active in 1996			2	7	5	7	6			3	3

SOURCE: U.S. Department of Labor, *Comparison of State Unemployment Insurance Laws*, National Foundation for Unemployment Corporation and Workers' Compensation, *Highlights of State Unemployment*, and Commerce Clearing House summaries of UI laws in individual states.

[a] Replacement rate is increased when trust fund balance falls below a set threshold.
[b] Employee tax diverted to Health Care Subsidy Fund from April 1996 through December 1997.

Although flexible benefits were authorized in 11 states in 1996, only one state (Maine) actually paid reduced benefits; trust fund balances exceeded trigger thresholds in the other 10. The fact that 14 states had an active solvency tax in 1996 indicates that benefit reduction features have lower thresholds than solvency taxes.

Forty-two UI programs have used at least one of the four solvency provisions shown in Tables 2-6 and 2-7. During 1996, 16 states had at least one active solvency provision, and 14 levied solvency taxes on employers.

According to such standard macroeconomic indicators as the overall unemployment rate, the economy was operating at or close to full employment in 1996: the unemployment rate for persons aged 16 and older was 5.4 percent of the labor force. If solvency taxes were activated in a year of full employment, how much added revenue would be generated from such taxes if the unemployment rate were much higher and trust funds were lower? One might have expected that four full years after 1992—the year of highest unemployment during the last recession—very few states would still be relying on solvency taxes. Presumably such taxes would be active only when funds were depleted by recession-related drawdowns. Since the recession of the early 1990s was mild in most areas of the country, the term "solvency tax" seems something of a misnomer.

In fact, many states have used solvency taxes more as a supplement to experience-rated taxes than as separate tax that is activated only in the event of a recession. Between 1988 and 1996, the number of UI programs that had solvency taxes varied from 29 to 32. Perhaps even more revealing is that the number of states with active solvency taxes ranged from a low of 10 in 1990 and 1991 to a high of 15 in 1994. On average, 11 UI programs had active solvency taxes from 1989 through 1992. During 1993–1996, after recession-related trust fund drawdowns, an average of 14 programs had active solvency taxes. These findings suggest that solvency taxes were only of modest importance during the last recession.

EMPIRICAL ANALYSES OF FLEXIBLE FINANCING

This section summarizes three empirical analyses of flexible financing. The first is a three-part study on tax responsiveness, using data going back to 1950 and covering 51 UI programs (Miller, Pavosevich, and Vroman 1997). The second is a simulation analysis of solvency taxes in six states. It uses simulation models that depict important aspects of the labor market, UI benefits, taxes, interest income, and trust fund balances in each state (Vroman 1990). The third is a model-based simulation of the UI financing system in Pennsylvania, following that state's adoption of flexible financing in 1988 (Worden and Vroman 1991a). All three studies use annual data.

Empirical Measures of Tax Responsiveness

The first analysis, of tax responsiveness, used data from 1950 to 1994.[18] To gauge the response of contributions to increased benefit outflows, we used one-, two-, and three-year responsiveness measures. Second, we looked at tax responsiveness in 1970 and 1990 for a subset of states that had recessions in both years. Third, we fitted regressions to estimate possible changes in tax responsiveness.

Since many states have added flexible financing in recent years, this analysis tested whether tax responsiveness increased measurably, particularly after the loan policy changes of the early 1980s. An important limitation is that the economy has had only one, fairly mild, recession since 1980–1983. There simply is not enough of a record from which to draw inferences.

Measures of tax responsiveness were based on annual data from 1950 through 1994. Recessions were identified on a state-by-state basis, rather than nationally, to capture differences in the timing of business cycles across states and differences in local economic downturns. Recessions were defined as periods when the increase in the benefit-cost rate (benefits as a percentage of total wages) from the base year to the trough year was at least 35 percent. The beginning year of the recession was identified as the first year in which benefits rose by 20 percent or more over the previous year (which then became the base year). To avoid overlapping response measures, recessions that began within three years of the previous recession were eliminated. The number of periods meeting all criteria totaled 303, or about 6 per state. Forty-seven occurred after 1982.

One-year, two-year, and three-year tax responses were then constructed for each recession. The one-year response is the ratio of the change in taxes divided by the change in benefits, with a lag of one year. The two-year response divided the sum of two years of tax changes by two-year benefit changes, again with a one-year lag between the first year of increased benefits and the first year of tax changes. The three-year response was similarly measured.[19]

Measuring tax responsiveness accurately presents some problems. First, benefit-cost rates frequently fluctuate, even when there is no recession; thus, tax rates are never fully in equilibrium. Second, the year-to-year pattern of benefit increases, (for example, slow buildup versus steep increase) has an effect on the measured response, except for the one-year measure. For example, for a given cumulative increase in benefits, the three-year measure would be higher for a recession in which the first year had the greatest increase than for one in which the increases started modestly and then gradually became greater. Third, the use of annual data obscures the precise timing of benefit increases.

Note that tax responses incorporate three elements—experience rating, solvency taxes, and legislative responses—and all affect tax revenues. Solvency taxes and legislative responses are likely to be proportionately more important for the two-year measure and especially important for the three-year measure.

When the individual state measures were examined, they revealed a wide range of values, including many outside the expected range of 0.0 to 1.0. In particular, there were many negative responses. It was assumed that extreme values are due to measurement problems, and extreme values were eliminated before any analysis took place. A recession was included only if all three measures fell within the range of acceptable values (including some negative values for the one-year and two-year measures). This restriction reduced the number of recessions to 236, with 33 occurring after 1982.

The first analysis examined the simple averages of tax responsiveness measures across states for 1952–1968, 1969–1981, and 1982–1991 (Table 2-8). There were no controls for state size or for other factors.

Table 2–8 Averages of Tax Responsiveness Measures

Beginning year	Number of downturns	R1, One-year response	R2, Two-year response	R3, Three-year response
1952–68	88	0.11	0.31	0.43
1969–81	115	0.14	0.36	0.54
1982–91	33	0.15	0.34	0.62

Four observations can be made about these averages. First, the period from 1952–1968 had the lowest average responsiveness for all three measures. Second, the 1982–1991 period had a clear edge over the 1969–1981 period only for the three-year measure and even fell slightly below it for the two-year measure. Third, the differences in responsiveness were the clearest between the first two periods, which suggests that most of the increase in responsiveness occurred during the 1970s and not the 1980s. Finally, the biggest gains in responsiveness were in the three-year measure.

The second analysis of tax responsiveness measures compared the 1990 recession to the 1970 recession. The 1970 recession predated the widespread financing problems experienced by the states in the mid 1970s and early-to-mid 1980s. A key difference between the 1970 and 1990 recessions was that aggregate reserves, as a percentage of total payroll, were almost twice as large in 1969 than in 1989 (see Table 1-1).

Twenty-three states met the criteria in both periods, and responsiveness measures for the two recessions were compared for each state. Among the states for which all three response measures were higher in one period than in the other, nine states were more responsive in 1970 than in 1990, and seven states were more responsive in 1990 than in 1970.

An important point to note is that the two recessions were significantly different in magnitude for many states, which may affect the comparisons (see Tables 1-2 and 1-3). Of the 12 states where there was both a clear difference in the severity of the two recessions and a clear difference in responsiveness, the financing systems in eight were more responsive in the milder of the two recessions.

The third analysis fitted a set of pooled regressions to control for factors that might affect measured responsiveness. All three responsiveness measures (R1, R2, and R3) were used as dependent variables. The explanatory variables included the reserve ratio at the beginning of the recession, the change in the benefit-cost rate for each year of the recession, and dummies for fixed state effects. Time effects were measured with two binary variables, one for after 1969 and one for years after 1982 (see Miller, Pavosevich, and Vroman [1997], Table 9.8).

The regressions show that responsiveness is clearly related to reserve levels, with greater responsiveness occurring in states having lower reserve ratios. The magnitude of this effect, however, is not very large. A 1-percentage-point drop in the reserve ratio had estimated effects that ranged from a 3-percentage-point increase in the one-year responsiveness measure to a 5- to 6-percentage-point increase in the three-year responsiveness measure.

None of the time dummies proved significant. The largest time coefficients, in fact, were negative, possibly indicating a reduction in tax responsiveness over time, after controlling for reserve levels.

The regressions and the other two analyses suggest that tax responsiveness has not increased since the early 1980s.

A Six-State Simulation Analysis of Solvency Taxes

In an earlier book, I examined the effectiveness of solvency taxes in preventing trust fund indebtedness in six large states.[20] My approach used state-level simulation models and paired simulations for 1988 to 1997. Within each pair, solvency taxes were either turned on and off. The simulations emphasized different experiences, based on each state's own unemployment and on national unemployment during the 1970s and the 1980s. Tax receipts, trust fund balances, and borrowing were noted for each simulation, and the differences between pairs showed the estimated effects of solvency taxes.

Four features were identified that affect the performance or effectiveness of solvency taxes: 1) the threshold trust fund level that activates the tax, 2) the range of statutory tax rates, 3) the proportion of employers affected, and 4) the possibility of negative as well as positive adjustments in solvency tax rate. Across the six states, the trust fund thresholds ranged from a high of 3.75 percent of covered wages in

Michigan to a low of a zero fund balance in New Jersey. The range of maximum statutory tax rate increases ranged from lows of 0.7 percent in New Jersey and 0.8 percent in California to highs of 3.0 percent in Michigan and 3.4 percent in Ohio.[21] When activated, a solvency tax may apply to all employers or only to selected employers, who are identified by the level of their reserve ratio or benefit ratio. Four states levied solvency taxes on all employers, while two taxed only selected employers. Four states used solvency taxes only to increase UI revenues, while two (Florida and Texas) lowered as well as increased total revenues using solvency taxes, i.e., their solvency taxes can have negative tax rates when trust fund balances are high.[22]

To examine the importance of solvency taxes, simulations were conducted in which solvency taxes were removed from each state's tax rate structure. The different scenarios included a baseline for each state in which the state's unemployment rate (the TUR) was maintained at a steady 5.5 percent from 1988 to 1997. No state required loans from the U.S. Treasury for either of its baseline simulations. In all six states where there were differences between the baselines when solvency taxes were on or off, the differences were small (see Vroman [1990], Table 4-7).

When the states were analyzed in terms of the unemployment rates during the 1970s and 1980s, the absence of solvency taxes increased the volume of borrowing and reduced the ending (1997) trust fund balance, except in Florida. However, decreases in total borrowing and increases in end balances were generally small. In New Jersey, which had the lowest solvency tax trigger (a zero fund balance), no simulation showed an effect. The greatest effect of solvency taxes was found in Ohio when, under the simulation, the state experienced a repetition of state TURs and national TURs from the 1980s. The removal of Ohio's solvency taxes raised total borrowing by more than $1.0 billion under both TUR paths and caused the 1997 trust fund balance to be nearly $2.0 billion lower. The effect on loans and the 1997 end balances was smaller in other states, with the effect in Michigan consistently second in magnitude to that in Ohio.[23]

Probably the most important finding of the simulations was that solvency taxes did not prevent insolvency in any of the six states. There were 24 non-baseline simulations (six states, with national and state TURs from the 1970s and 1980s), and states needed loans in 7 of the 24. For all seven simulations, borrowing occurred both when the solvency tax was on and when it was off. The solvency tax modestly reduced the volume of borrowing, but it did not prevent indebtedness.

Solvency taxes proved of limited importance for the six states. In Ohio, where the effect was largest, borrowing was reduced by $1.1 to $1.3 billion and the end balance increased by $1.2 to $1.9 billion over the 10 years. The results indicate a serious recession would require discretionary action or stronger solvency tax provisions to increase the total response of UI taxes and to reduce the volume of borrowing. If solvency taxes are to have greater effect than that found in these simulations, they would need to include a more aggressive combination of higher trigger thresholds, a wider potential range of tax rates, and application to all employers.

Flexible Financing in Pennsylvania

During the late 1980s, UI officials in Illinois and Pennsylvania advocated flexible financing for their programs. A quantitative analysis of the Illinois 1987 law conducted at the Urban Institute, however, concluded that most of the improvement in solvency was achieved by two "permanent" provisions that are not really flexible. In the first, a fund-building tax of 0.4 percent was levied on employers. This tax has remained in place and used the same tax rate through 1996. In the second, the average weekly wage (AWW) used to make indexed increases to the maximum weekly benefit was redefined. The redefined AWW was 20 percent lower than the actual statewide AWW. There were other flexibility features in the Illinois law (including a provision to freeze the maximum WBA, as indicated in Table 2-7), but their effects on trust fund revenues and benefit outlays were distinctly secondary when compared to the two "permanent" revisions. Thus, it seems more accurate to consider Pennsylvania's 1988 law as the best example of a flexible financing law.

An analysis by Worden and Vroman (1991a) simulated the impact of flexible financing provisions in Pennsylvania's 1988 law. The law was designed to increase the automatic responsiveness of taxes and benefits, thus reducing the need for borrowing during recessions. The 1988 law followed earlier solvency laws in 1980 and 1983 and a history of large-scale borrowing from the U.S. Treasury.[24] Of the 37 state

UI programs that borrowed sometime during the 1970s and 1980s, Pennsylvania's $5.5 billion total was the largest.

Pennsylvania's 1988 solvency provisions provided for additional employer taxes, variable employee taxes, and benefit reductions. All adjustments to taxes and benefits are activated by a single trigger. That trigger is calculated as the ratio of the fund balance at the end of the current fiscal year (June 30th) to the average benefit amount for the current and the two previous fiscal years, with the ratio measured as a percentage.

There are two flexible employer taxes. An employer surcharge is imposed as a flat amount that can assume seven different values. Trigger ratio percentages of 150 or larger (trigger-level seven) cause a tax reduction. The largest surcharge is levied when the trigger percentage falls below 50 (trigger-level one). Employers are also subject to graduated "additional contributions" when the trigger percentage falls below 95. There is also a trigger-activated employee surcharge with a range of possible values from 0.0 to 0.2 percent of total covered wages. Finally, weekly benefits (for claimants paid above half the maximum WBA) drop by 5 percent whenever the trigger ratio falls below 50. Pennsylvania's flexible financing provisions specify effects as fixed dollar amounts. Thus, as economic growth occurs, the size of these effects automatically declines relative to statewide macroeconomic variables such as covered employment and total wages.

The effects of these automatic provisions were studied using a simulation model that included detailed equations for determining UI taxes and UI benefits.[25] Model simulations were conducted for the years 1991 to 1999. The analysis specified a series of unemployment/inflation scenarios and simulated benefits, taxes, and trust fund balances with the flexible financing provisions first off and then on. The simulations also used state unemployment rates from earlier periods and specified successively higher rates of unemployment. Simulations with differing inflation rates were also conducted.

Each simulation tracked total benefit outlays, tax receipts, borrowing from the U.S. Treasury, and the trust fund end balance for the nine years. Differences in total borrowing were noted for paired simulations that differed only in the flexible financing provisions being on or off. For each pair, the simulation with flexible financing on had a higher time path for the trust fund balance and less total borrowing.

However, the most serious recessions caused large-scale borrowing to occur even in the simulations with flexible financing on.

Perhaps the most interesting results were produced by a series of simulations that raised the average total unemployment rate by increments of 0.5 percentage points. Total benefit outlays grew consistently for increments to the TUR. However, the added taxes and reduced benefits reached their upper limits, causing the fund balance to fall further and cumulative borrowing to rise, despite flexible financing. Even when all provisions were fully turned on, benefit outflows exceeded taxes by wide margins.

The distribution of sacrifices by workers and by employers were sensitive to the assumed rate of inflation.[26] At low rates of inflation, the burden of flexible financing was roughly 50:50, with most of the employee share arising from employee taxes. At higher rates of inflation, the employee share rose to more than half, with employee taxes still accounting for most of the increased employee share. This finding is a direct consequence of the limitation on employer taxes caused by the fixed tax base. The tax base for employees, however, is unlimited. Additional simulations suggest that indexing both the employer tax base and other solvency provisions (rather than using fixed absolute dollar amounts) would substantially improve the effectiveness of flexible financing in preventing indebtedness and in reducing the scale of insolvency.

Four of the principal findings of the simulations are straightforward.

1. Pennsylvania's flexible financing provisions reduced its scale of borrowing but did not prevent insolvency.

2. Flexible financing was more effective in small downturns than in more serious recessions (measured in terms of the increase in the average total rate of unemployment for 1991–1999).

3. Inflation weakened the effectiveness of flexible financing in the later years of the period simulated.

4. Indexing the employer tax base and the trigger would remedy most of the effects of high inflation.

However, flexible financing could not forestall large-scale borrowing during periods of high unemployment, even when the system was fully indexed. Tax increases and/or benefit reductions would require more "bite" to prevent large-scale indebtedness during a major recession.

Pennsylvania benefited from its flexible financing during the 1990–1992 recession. Following two consecutive years of 1.5 percent employer tax reductions (1990 and 1991) under the highest of the seven trigger thresholds, there were five consecutive years of higher taxes. The thresholds were number five in 1992, number three in 1993 and 1994, number four in 1995, and number five in 1996.[27] The maximum solvency taxes levied during 1993 and 1994 raised the employer levy by 14.74 percent, while employees paid a 0.15 percent employee payroll tax on total wages. By the end of 1996, the state's trust fund stood at $2.03 billion. Its reserve ratio for 1996 was 1.78 percent, essentially the same as at the end of 1990, a year that flexible financing actually reduced employer taxes.

The downturn of the early 1990s was comparatively mild in Pennsylvania. The state's TUR averaged 7.2 percent during 1991–1993, compared with an average of 5.0 percent during 1988–1990. Benefit payouts during 1991–1993 averaged $1.57 billion, or 1.65 percent of covered wages. Average payouts during 1991–1993 were about 70 percent higher than during 1988–1990; however, payouts during 1991–1993 were not especially high by historic standards. From 1970 through 1989, benefit payout rates exceeded 1.65 percent in 7 years and exceeded 1.50 percent in 11 years. The 1991–1993 downturn was comparatively mild in terms of Pennsylvania's history.

On the other hand, note that Pennsylvania did not need to draw on the full potential of its flexible financing system for a single year during 1992–1996. In the face of a single, albeit mild, recession, flexible financing successfully accomplished its purpose in Pennsylvania.

SOME FINAL COMMENTS ON FLEXIBLE FINANCING

In deciding whether to follow a funding strategy with a strong element of flexible financing, it is important for a state to look at the trade-offs. The chief argument in favor of flexible financing is that trust fund reserves can be kept low and the risk of borrowing can simultaneously be minimized. The negative aspects of large balances have been stressed, in recent years, especially by employers. Some state officials also judge that the "opportunity cost" of holding balances exceeds the interest earnings on reserves. For any given level of benefit payouts, a state may prefer to hold smaller trust fund balances than it would have in the past, on the grounds that the rate of return is higher for funds held by employers.[28] Second, large trust fund balances may lead to pressures for liberalizing benefits or for diverting UI taxes to other uses. Either use of the trust fund is easier to argue politically if the fund balance is perceived to be larger than necessary.[29]

It is clear that, in the aggregate, states now have smaller desired trust fund levels than in the past. Although pre-recession balances in 1989 were high relative to those of the 1970s, they were only about half of 1969 balances.[30] (This is an appropriate comparison because both 1969 and 1989 fell at the end of long periods of economic growth, and that growth presumably allowed state trust funds to rise to desired levels.)

A second impetus towards flexible financing is that, even if a state chooses to have a low trust fund balance, there are disincentives that encourage a state to avoid or minimize borrowing. Since 1982, interest has been charged on loans (except those repaid the year they are made). The interest must be paid from sources outside the trust fund, either from a separate tax or from a state's general revenues. A further disincentive is the automatic repayment provision in the FUTA tax, a provision which is activated after two years of borrowing. The FUTA tax repays the loan through a flat surcharge on the low federal tax base, rather than through the experience-rated state UI tax.

The chief argument against flexible financing is that the timing of benefit decreases and tax increases hurts both claimants and employers. Claimants suffer reduced benefits at a time when their need is greatest. Businesses undergo tax increases before they have fully recovered from the recession. The traditional rationale for forward or advance funding rests on the argument that such adjustments should not be occurring at such times or should, at least, be minimized.

Two additional arguments against relying on flexible financing should also be noted. First, a state may implement flexible financing but the provisions may not be strong enough to prevent insolvency.

Flexible tax provisions, for example, simply may not generate enough additional revenue in time to counteract the effects of a serious recession. The simulations reported above indicate that this is the case for Pennsylvania, even though the state did not have financing problems during or after the 1990–1992 downturn. Second, there may not enough political will to let strong flexible financing operate as intended. When the time comes, the state's executive and/or its legislature might decide to nullify the automatic response to satisfy preferences of claimants or businesses, or both. Without a large trust fund reserve, a state may find it needs large-scale loans. The result may be a legislated, discretionary, pay-as-you-go response brought in during a crisis, rather than the automatic pay-as-you-go response advocated by proponents of flexible financing.

From a national perspective, even if individual states find flexible financing an attractive option, its widespread use would be cause for concern. In national terms, the main problem with flexible financing is that it reduces the counter-cyclical performance of the UI system. One of the original objectives of the UI system was that it act as an automatic stabilizer of the macroeconomy, primarily by maintaining consumer purchasing power. Flexible benefit provisions undercut this stabilizing effect. Taxes that respond too quickly may cut business spending at the wrong time and harm the recovery. The long-term decline in the proportion of the unemployed who receive benefits has already diminished the stabilizing role of the UI. The increased use of flexible financing would further erode UI's stabilizing role.

During the 1950s, when UI trust fund balances were much more substantial, there was a great deal of debate about and experimentation with ways to make tax rates more counter-cyclical. In the past 10 or 15 years, a time of relatively low trust fund balances, there has been a significant shift in the opposite direction, towards a more immediate recovery of benefit costs through flexible financing.

In any event, it appears that the shift towards flexible financing is not yet of sufficient importance to have a large quantitative effect. This conclusion emerges both from an analysis of UI statutes and from the empirical studies reviewed in this chapter.

Notes

1. The two main sources used throughout this chapter are *Comparison of State Unemployment Insurance Laws* (U.S. Department of Labor 1996) and *Highlights of State Unemployment Compensation Laws* (National Foundation for Unemployment Compensation and Workers' Compensation 1996). The *Comparison* and its predecessors has been published for roughly 50 years, while *Highlights* has been available since 1982. Both use information assembled by the staff of the UI Service, with the *Highlights* being less comprehensive but more readily accessible.
2. Other experience-rating features of potential interest include the number of experience-rating schedules, the range of triggers that the schedules encompass, and the average distance between schedules (the change in the tax rate for an employer in a given experience-rating category when the rate moves from one schedule to the next). Changes in noncharging (benefit payments not assigned to an individual employer) and ineffective charging (failure to assign a benefit charge because the employer is already paying the maximum tax rate) could also be important.
3. Payments in Massachusetts are due on the fifteenth of the month following the end of each quarter.
4. In a reserve-ratio state, this would mean a lower reserve ratio (reserves as a percentage of covered payrolls), while in a benefit-ratio state this would be a higher benefit ratio (charged benefits as a percentage of covered payrolls).
5. Note that a second effect arises from moving to a higher tax schedule once the fund balance decreases.
6. Aggregate net reserves decreased from $10.5 billion (at the end of 1974) to $1.0 billion (at the end of 1977) and from $8.6 billion (at the end of 1979) to –$5.8 billion (at the end of 1983). The most recent drawdown, shown in Table 1-4, was from $36.9 billion (at the end of 1989) to $25.8 billion (at the end of 1992).
7. An even wider range of maximum rates would appear if the maximums from the highest state tax rate schedules were shown rather than the actual rates in effect.
8. For completeness, note that benefit-wage ratios are used in two states (Delaware and Oklahoma) and payroll declines are used in one state (Alaska). These experience-rating systems operate much like benefit-ratio systems.
9. All five states in which the TWP was higher in 1996 than in 1986 have indexed tax bases.
10. For other programs, the trigger changed in ways that left the direction of the change unclear. In Kansas, for example, the 1986 top schedule trigger was a fund balance reserve ratio of less than 1.5 percent. In 1996, however, Kansas had no explicit trigger for its top schedule because it no longer had a set of explicit schedules. Employers with a negative balance were taxed up to a top rate of 6.4 percent, while the top rate was 5.4 percent for others.
11. The estimate of tax capacity for 1996 uses the TWP from 1995. Since the TWP has shown a downward trend in nonindexed states, the 1996 estimates overstate the tax capacity of most states.

12. In California, the solvency tax is levied as an additional 15 percent on the highest experience-rated schedule.
13. Prior to 1980, federal legislation had twice prevented automatic tax increases in states with long-term trust fund debts. The increases would have raised the federal tax component of UI taxes in these states (see Vroman [1986], Chapter 1).
14. New Hampshire has an emergency tax of 0.5 percent that can be activated when the UI commissioner determines that an emergency exists.
15. Eight of the nine that brought in solvency taxes in the 1970s also borrowed from the U.S. Treasury during the 1970s, and five had loans that equaled or exceeded 1.0 percent of covered payrolls in 1975 (Connecticut, Hawaii, Michigan, Pennsylvania, and Rhode Island). See Vroman (1986), Table 3-1.
16. Note that New Jersey's employee tax was diverted to another purpose from April 1996 through December 1997.
17. The three elements of the Illinois trigger are the level of the trust fund, the average employer tax rates, and the growth in the payment of initial claims.
18. This analysis is described in Miller, Pavosevich, and Vroman (1997). Mike Miller and Robert Pavosevich of the U.S. Labor Department's UI Service did the analysis.
19. In formulas:
    $R1 = (Tax_t - Tax_{t-1}) / (Ben_{t-1} - Ben_{t-2})$.
    $R2 = [(Tax_{t+1} - Tax_{t-1}) + (Tax_t - Tax_{t-1})] / [(Ben_t - Ben_{t-2}) + (Ben_{t-1} - Ben_{t-2})]$.
    $R3 = [(Tax_{t+2} - Tax_{t-1}) + (Tax_{t+1} - Tax_{t-1}) + (Tax_t - Tax_{t-1})] / [(Ben_{t+1} - Ben_{t-2}) + (Ben_t - Ben_{t-2}) + (Ben_{t-1} - Ben_{t-2})]$.
    "Tax" represents annual UI tax receipts; "Ben" stands for annual benefit payments; and the subscripts refer to periods measured from the current year.
20. See Vroman (1990), pp. 106–111. The six states were New Jersey, Michigan, Ohio, Florida, Texas, and California.
21. The maximum solvency rates for both the Ohio and Michigan simulations were higher than shown in Table 2-6. The higher solvency tax rates that had applied before 1988 were used in the simulations. Thus, for both states, the maximum effects of solvency taxes would be smaller if the analysis were repeated using the solvency taxes of 1996.
22. The solvency tax in Florida was its fund balance adjustment factor, part of the variable adjustment factor in the state's tax structure. Unlike the other states, the tax is part of experience-rated taxes in Florida.
23. This consistent one-two ranking for Ohio and Michigan also appeared when taxes and other financing variables were measured in absolute levels and as percentages of covered wages.
24. Pennsylvania's earlier law is described in Vroman (1986), Chapter 2.
25. The model's equations are shown in Worden and Vroman (1991a), Appendix A.
26. Sacrifices by workers have two potential components: increased employee taxes and reduced benefits to claimants.
27. See Worden and Vroman (1991a) for the detailed tax and benefit provisions which were activated under each of the seven thresholds.

28. There is no significant research showing comparative rate of return calculations to buttress the presumption that rates of return are higher on employer-controlled assets, but the presumption is probably correct. Arguments to reduce UI taxes on employers that emphasized this differential would be weakened if UI trust funds were invested in a broader range of assets than federal government debt.

29. Again, rhetoric and casual observation provide much of the basis for this assertion. It would be useful to investigate the issue in a formal statistical (regression) framework.

30. See Table 1-1. See also Miller, Pavosevich, and Vroman (1997), Table 9.1.

3 Tax-Base Indexing

Eighteen UI programs tie the taxable wage base to the average weekly wage in covered employment. This chapter focuses on the experiences of those states and compares them with the remaining states, in which the tax-base changes must be explicitly legislated. The chapter is divided into two sections. The first describes the main features of tax-base indexing. The second studies some effects of tax-base indexing with an emphasis on two groupings of the states, those with indexed tax bases and those with fixed tax bases. The second section includes comparative analyses of trends in tax capacity and tax rates, as well as analyses of performance over time and during the recessionary phase of the business cycle.

AN OVERVIEW OF TAX-BASE INDEXING

Persistent growth in money wages is a ubiquitous feature of market economies. During the 1990s, money wage growth has been low by historical standards, but the average weekly wage in UI-covered employment has grown in each year. From 1990 through 1996, the annual percentage growth in the AWW for taxable covered employers ranged from a low of 1.5 percent (1993) to a high of 5.6 percent (1992). The cumulative growth in the AWW during those years was 28.1 percent, or from $428.02 in 1989 to $548.17 in 1996.

Roughly two-thirds of state UI programs set their taxable wage base through discretionary action, raising it only periodically, and typically setting the tax base only slightly higher than the minimum base mandated by the federal tax base conformity requirement. The federally mandated taxable wage base has been $7,000 since 1983. In 1996, 12 states had tax bases of $7,000, 20 had tax bases between $7,001 and $10,000, and 21 had tax bases above $10,000.

Low tax bases are characteristic of many large states. Taxable covered employment exceeded 3.0 million in seven states during 1995. Three of the seven (California, Florida, and New York) had tax bases of

$7,000 in 1996, while the other four (Illinois, Ohio, Pennsylvania, and Texas) had tax bases of either $8,000 or $9,000.

Low taxable wage bases are strongly associated with low taxable wage proportions. For the 12 states with $7,000 tax bases in 1996, the average TWP was 0.270, compared with the national average of 0.342. These 12 UI programs accounted for 33.9 percent of covered wages in 1996. For states in which the 1996 tax bases ranged from $7,001 to $10,000, the TWP averaged 0.328, while the TWP averaged 0.472 for states where the tax base exceeded $10,000. The latter two groups accounted for 42.6 percent and 23.6 percent of covered wages, respectively. States with high taxable wage bases had much higher TWPs, but they were generally smaller states and accounted for about 40 percent of all UI programs (21 of 53) but only 23.6 percent of covered wages. As shown below, states with high tax bases are disproportionately the states with indexed tax bases.

Theoretically, a state could achieve a high taxable wage base either through discretionary action or through tax-base indexing. In practice, states with fixed tax bases have not raised their bases in line with the growth in average wages. Taxable wages have persistently tended to grow more slowly than total covered wages, and the TWP has tended to decline in most states. For example, between 1989 and 1996, total wages for taxable covered employers grew by 40.7 percent. Over the same period, taxable wages grew by only 25.1 percent. Nationwide, the TWP declined from 0.385 in 1989 to 0.342 in 1996.

The decrease in the TWP between 1989 and 1996 is a continuation of a long-term trend that goes back to 1940. Annual changes in the TWP were negative in 49 of the 56 years between 1941 and 1996. The federal taxable wage base increased three times during that time, from $3,000 to $4,200 in 1972, to $6,000 in 1978, and to $7,000 in 1983. Three of the years when the TWP increased were years when the federal tax base was raised: the increases in the TWP were 0.064 in 1972, 0.046 in 1978, and 0.024 in 1983. The four other years when TWP increased were 1945, 1976, 1993, and 1994. Those increases were all small,[1] and for 1976, 1993, and 1994 they reflect recession-related state action that raised tax bases in several states. The increases were large enough to offset the persistent tendency for TWP to decrease.[2] Fixed tax bases in the majority of states have been the most important factor causing the long-term decline in the TWP. The nationwide decrease was from 0.928 in 1940 to 0.342 in 1996. In 1996, only about one-third of covered wages were taxable. In New York, a high-wage state with a $7,000 tax base, the TWP was only 0.213 in 1996.

Increases in prices and wages have two important effects on UI programs. The discussion to this point has emphasized only the effect on the TWP when a state has a fixed tax base or adjusts its tax base only through legislation. Legislated adjustments have generally been too small to keep the TWP constant. Over time, UI programs must raise revenues from ever-declining proportions of covered wages.

The second important effect of rising wages is to erode benefit payment levels relative to pre-unemployment wages. All states limit the maximum weekly benefit amount. If the maximum WBA is not periodically adjusted upward, an increasing share of recipients will be paid the maximum, and the average benefit replacement rate (average weekly benefits as a proportion of average weekly wages) will fall over time. National data and data from individual states, however, show that UI replacement rates have been remarkably stable. The national average replacement rate was 0.361 for the 27 years between 1970 and 1996. The annual replacement rate was between 0.354 and 0.372 for all but three of those years. Over the same time, the TWP decreased from 0.477 to 0.342, despite three increases in the federal taxable wage base.

Fifty-two of the 53 UI programs follow one of three approaches in adjusting the maximum weekly benefit and taxable wage base. During 1996, there were 17 UI programs in which both the tax base and the maximum WBA were explicitly tied, through indexing, to average wages; 19 programs with indexed changes in the maximum WBA but not the tax base; and 16 in which neither was indexed. The remaining program (Alaska) indexed its UI tax base but not its maximum WBA. The shares of overall covered wages for these programs in 1995 were as follows: both the tax base and the maximum WBA indexed, 0.167; the tax base nonindexed but the maximum WBA indexed, 0.384; neither indexed, 0.447; and the tax base indexed but the maximum WBA fixed, 0.002. Thus, roughly 83 percent of covered wages were found in states without an indexed tax base. The 18 states with an indexed tax base accounted for only 16.9 percent of covered wages. States with indexed maximum WBAs accounted for 55.1 percent of covered wages. On average, tax-base indexing was present in small states.

Twice as many programs use indexed maximum WBAs as use indexed tax bases, 36 versus 18 in 1996. The indexing of the maximum WBAs also occurred earlier. The first state to index its maximum WBA was Kansas, in the early 1950s. By 1966, 15 UI programs had indexed maximum WBAs and just one (Hawaii) had an indexed tax base. The numbers increased to 30 and 3, respectively, in 1975. By 1986, there were 35 states with indexed maximum WBAs and 18 with indexed tax bases. Thus, most states with an indexed maximum WBA adopted the provision between the mid 1950s and mid 1970s, but the adoption of indexed tax bases occurred mainly between the mid 1970s and the mid 1980s. Since the mid 1980s, the prevalence of either kind of indexing has not changed in any important way.[3]

The number of UI programs with indexed tax bases has remained constant at 18 since 1986, with no state adding or discontinuing indexing. Details of these states' indexing provisions are shown in Table 3-1. Note that both Montana and Washington experimented with fixed annual tax base increases before adopting explicit indexing formulas that tie the tax base to lagged average wages. Most states that have adopted indexing did so between 1975 and 1986. Often, this was part of solvency legislation motivated by the trust fund financing problems of 1975–1977 or 1980–1983. Each state that adopted tax-base indexing has retained it.

The 18 states with indexed tax bases are generally small and generally lie west of the Mississippi River. Their programs accounted for 16.9 percent of covered wages and 17.7 percent of covered employment in 1996. Employment in those states averaged 931,000 in 1996, compared with 2,227,000 in nonindexed states. Only four (Minnesota, New Jersey, North Carolina, and Washington) had total employment that exceeded 1,787,000, the national average for state-level covered employment, in 1996. Fourteen states with indexing lie west of the Mississippi River. However, because California and Texas have not indexed their tax bases, the 14 represent only about 29 percent of employment in the 24 western states.[4] Indexing is less common in the East, and the four states with indexed tax bases (out of 29 programs) accounted for only 11 percent of UI-covered employment in 1996.

The percentage of indexing ranges from 100 percent of annual wages (Hawaii and Idaho) to 50 percent (North Carolina and Oklahoma). Six programs have changed their percentage, with increases

Table 3-1 Tax-Base Indexing in Individual States through 1996

	Indexing				1996		Taxable wage proportion (TWP)		TWP rank, 1995
	First year	% of annual wage	Years in effect	Lag (months)	Tax base	Tax base rank	1986	1996	
Alaska	1981	75	1983–96	18	24,400	2	0.681	0.654	4
		60	1981–82						
Hawaii	1965	100	1977–96	18	25,800	1	0.686	0.711	1
		90	1965–76						
Idaho	1976	100	1976–96	24	21,600	3	0.693	0.673	3
Iowa	1978	66.7	1978–96	12	14,700	12	0.582	0.531	13
Minnesota	1982	60	1982–96	12	15,800	11	0.471	0.477	15
Montana	1979	80	1986–96	12	15,800	10	0.714	0.686	2
		75	1979–85[a]						
Nevada	1975	66.7	1975–96	12	16,600	9	0.590	0.579	8
New Jersey	1976	53.8	1976–96	24	18,000	6	0.456	0.458	17
New Mexico	1978	65	1978–96	18	13,900	14	0.549	0.541	12
North Carolina	1984	50	1995–96	12	11,600	17	0.515	0.455	19
		60	1984–94						
North Dakota	1979	70	1979–96	18	13,900	15	0.567	0.548	11
Oklahoma	1986	50	1986–96	12	10,900	19	0.462	0.457	18
Oregon	1976	80	1976–96	24	20,000	5	0.629	0.607	5
Rhode Island	1980	70	1980–96	12	17,000	8	0.554	0.556	10

(continued)

82

Table 3-1 (continued)

| | Indexing | | | 1996 | | Taxable wage proportion (TWP) | | TWP rank, 1995 |
	First year	% of annual wage	Years in effect	Lag (months)	Tax base	Tax base rank	1986	1996	
Utah	1977	75	1985–96	18	17,200	7	0.576	0.575	9
		100	1977–81[b]						
Virgin Islands	1985	60	1995–96	18	13,900	13	0.778	0.590	6
		100	1985–94						
Washington	1971	80	1989–96	24	20,300	4	0.532	0.584	7
			1971–88[c]						
Wyoming	1984	55	1984–96	24	12,100	16	0.508	0.485	14

[a] Maximum increase in tax base limited to $200 per year from 1979 to 1985.
[b] Tax base frozen at $12,000 from 1981 to 1983 and increased to $13,300 in 1984.
[c] Tax base increased by $1,200 in 1972, by $600 per year from 1973 to 1984, and by 15 percent above the previous year's value from 1986 to 1988.

occurring in Alaska, Hawaii, and Montana but decreases occurring in North Carolina, Utah, and the Virgin Islands. Two of those decreases occurred in 1995. The lags between changes in the average annual wages of the reference period and the tax base increase range from 12 to 24 months.

Indexing has raised taxable wage bases considerably above the federal taxable wage base. The lowest tax base for the 18 programs in 1986 was $10,900 in Oklahoma. The 1996 tax base equaled or exceeded $20,000 in five indexed states (Alaska, Hawaii, Idaho, Oregon, and Washington), while it was between $15,000 and $19,900 in another five (Montana, Nevada, New Jersey, Rhode Island, and Utah). The 17 highest UI tax bases in 1995 were in indexed states, while the tax base in the remaining indexed state (Oklahoma) ranked 19th.

Recall from the earlier discussion that 21 states had tax bases above $10,000 in 1996. The three nonindexed states in this group and their tax bases were Connecticut ($11,000), Massachusetts ($10,800), and Wisconsin ($10,500). In the early 1990s, Connecticut and Massachusetts had financing problems that led to increases in their taxable wage bases. Because of those increases, Connecticut's 1996 tax base was the only one in a nonindexed state that exceeded the tax base of any of the 18 indexed states, and that was only by $100 ($11,000 versus Oklahoma's $10,900). In short, indexing has been the means whereby individual states have achieved high tax bases.

The high tax bases in the indexed states are associated with high taxable wage proportions. In 1996, the TWPs in these states ranged from 0.711 to 0.455, compared with the national average of 0.342 and an average of 0.306 in nonindexed states. Note also that the lowest TWPs among the indexed states were found in Oklahoma and North Carolina, states whose indexing percentages were lowest, at 50 percent of lagged average annual earnings. The average TWP across the indexed states was 0.519 in 1996, essentially identical to the average percentage of 0.523 in 1986 (see Table 2-5).

The final column in Table 3-1 shows the 1995 rankings of TWPs across the 53 UI programs. Of the 19 highest rankings, 18 were in states with indexed tax bases.[5] The 1996 TWP rankings are similar. Indexing the tax base has resulted in high TWPs.

For most states in Table 3-1, the TWPs for 1986 and 1996 are quite similar. Decreases occurred in North Carolina and the Virgin Islands, two states that reduced their indexing percentages in 1995. The large change in Washington can be attributed to use of a system for changing the tax base between 1986 and 1988 that differed from the one used in later years. The indexing percentage was effectively lower than 80 percent in 1986, but since there were 15 percent annual tax-base increases during 1986–1988, one would expect a higher TWP after 1988.

For 11 of the remaining 15 states in Table 3-1, the TWP was lower in 1996 than in 1986. This may reflect growing inequality in earnings during the period when workers towards the top of the wage distribution range realized above average wage gains. This inference is consistent with other data on annual earnings but cannot be verified here since the TWP estimates are based on aggregate (rather than on micro) data.

Recall from Table 2-5 that the TWP in nonindexed states fell markedly between 1986 and 1996, from 0.386 to 0.306. By 1996, the average TWP in nonindexed states averaged only 0.590 of the average TWP in indexed ones. The implications this has for tax capacity, effective UI tax rates, and maintaining trust fund reserves are examined in the next section.

To summarize, 18 states have indexed taxable wage bases. Sixteen of the 18 adopted indexation between 1975 and 1986. The percentage of indexing—the tax base as a percentage of lagged average annual wages—ranges from 50 percent to 100 percent across those jurisdictions. Between 1986 and 1996, the taxable wage proportion remained virtually unchanged in the indexed states, but it dropped markedly in the nonindexed states.

SOME EFFECTS OF TAX-BASE INDEXING

An indexed tax base can affect a UI program's financing, both in the long run and during recessions. This section investigates four issues: 1) UI tax capacity, 2) the distribution of tax rates along tax rate schedules, 3) maintaining reserves in the long run, and 4) maintaining reserves during recessions. The analysis focuses on the period after 1986, a period with no change in the number of indexed and nonindexed programs.

Maintaining Tax Capacity

Tax capacity, as defined in Chapter 2, is the product of the taxable wage proportion and the average tax rate for the top tax rate schedule. Besides the taxes implied by a state's top experience-rating schedule, about half the states also have solvency taxes. The contribution of solvency taxes to a UI program's total tax capacity is the product of the TWP and the average rate for its solvency tax. Since solvency taxes are often levied at a single rate, their contribution to total tax capacity is easy to calculate.

Total tax capacity is defined by the following expression:

Eq. 3-1 $TCap = TWP(TRTop + TRSolv)$,

where   TCap is tax capacity,
TWP is the taxable wage proportion,
TRTop is the average tax rate on the top tax schedule, and
TRSolv is the average tax rate for the solvency tax.

The tax rates in Eq. 3-1 are often expressed as percentages, as in Tables 2-2 through 2-5.

There is an ambiguity in expression Eq. 3-1 that merits discussion. The average tax rate for the top tax schedule (TRTop) depends both on the progression of rates between the minimum and the maximum rates and on the distribution of employers and their taxable wages across individual tax rate categories. The distribution of employers changes at different stages of the business cycle. After a recession, a higher fraction of taxable wages will be concentrated near the maximum rate, but after a long expansion, more will be concentrated towards the minimum rate. Moving to a higher schedule will cause the average tax rate to increase, not only because higher rates are in effect for each experience category but also because relatively more taxable wages will be located in categories near the maximum tax rate.

The difficulty can be avoided if states use array allocations to set employer rates along a given tax rate schedule. Each schedule has a fixed number of categories (for example, 20 in Washington), but taxable wages in each category are equalized (5 percent in Washington). Employers are ranked on the state's experience indicator (benefit ratios in Washington). Cumulative distributions (from low to high) then determine the tax rate for each employer. Within each rate category, employers are taxed at a single tax rate. Because the percentages of taxable wages in each category are controlled, the average tax rate across all categories is also known, regardless of the distribution of employer-experience indicators. Using array allocations allows a state to make more accurate revenue projections because the average tax rate can be projected with a high degree of accuracy.[6]

In states that do not use array allocations, the assessment of tax capacity can be inaccurate because the average tax rate for the top schedule is not precisely determined. The estimates shown in Table 2-5, for example, probably understate the tax capacity for experience-rated taxes, because the procedure did not allow the average tax rate for the top schedule to increase relative to the simple average of the minimum and maximum rates.

Regardless of this shortcoming, it is clear that a decrease in the TWP reduces a state's tax capacity. Between 1986 and 1996, the TWP fell in nonindexed states while it remained constant in indexed states. Nor did the average statutory rate for the top experience-rated schedule increase much between 1986 and 1996. Thus, for experience-rated taxes, tax capacity did not decline in indexed states, but it did decline in nonindexed states.

Table 3-2 shows state-level estimates of total tax capacity in 1986 and 1996, including solvency taxes. The columns for each year show the four separate elements of Eq. 3-1 for total capacity. Table 3-2 also shows the maximum tax rate from the top tax schedule. In each state with a solvency tax, the tax was assumed to be turned on. Where a range of solvency rates is possible, the average solvency tax rate is estimated the same way as the average experience-rated tax rate—as the simple average of the minimum and maximum solvency tax rates. The states are identified according to the presence or absence of tax-base indexing.

The measures of total tax capacity shown in Table 3-2 closely resemble those in Table 2-5. In other words, most of the UI tax capacity is generated by experience-rated taxes. The national tax rate averages in 1986 were 3.72 percent for experience-rated taxes in the top schedule and 0.64 percent for solvency taxes. Solvency taxes accounted for just under 15 percent of total tax capacity in 1986 and for about 14 percent in 1996.

Table 3-2 Total Tax Capacity for the Top Rated Tax Schedules Plus Solvency Taxes, 1986 and 1996

State	1986					1996				
		Top schedule		Top			Top schedule		Top	
	TWP	Max. rate (%)	Avg. rate (%)	solv. tax rate (%)	Total tax capacity (%)	TWP	Max. rate (%)	Avg. rate (%)	solv. tax rate (%)	Total tax capacity (%)
Alabama	0.460	5.4	2.95	0.70	1.68	0.352	6.8	3.73		1.31
Alaska[a]	0.681	6.5	3.75	0.75	3.06	0.654	6.5	3.75	0.75	2.94
Arizona	0.405	5.4	4.15		1.68	0.316	5.4	4.15		1.31
Arkansas	0.477	6.0	3.05	1.00	1.93	0.426	6.0	3.05	0.80	1.64
California	0.353	5.4	3.35	0.50	1.36	0.250	5.4	3.35	0.50	0.96
Colorado	0.415	5.4	3.05		1.27	0.383	5.4	2.75	0.55	1.26
Connecticut	0.324	6.4	3.95	1.00	1.60	0.305	6.9	4.45	1.50	1.81
Delaware	0.402	7.0	3.55	2.00	2.23	0.300	8.0	4.05	2.00	1.82
District of Columbia	0.351	5.4	3.10	0.90	1.40	0.267	7.4	4.65		1.24
Florida	0.428	5.4	2.75		1.18	0.319	5.4	2.75		0.88
Georgia	0.412	5.7	3.21	1.62	1.99	0.331	8.1	4.08	1.35	1.80
Hawaii[a]	0.686	5.4	4.00	1.20	3.57	0.711	5.4	3.90		2.77
Idaho[a]	0.693	6.8	4.85		3.36	0.673	6.8	4.85		3.26
Illinois	0.378	6.6	3.40	0.60	1.51	0.303	6.6	3.40	0.60	1.21
Indiana	0.372	5.4	3.35		1.25	0.293	5.7	3.55		1.04
Iowa[a]	0.582	7.0	3.75		2.18	0.531	9.0	4.50		2.39
Kansas	0.483	5.4	2.71		1.31	0.416	6.4	3.20		1.33

Table 3-2 (continued)

State	1986					1996				
	TWP	Top schedule Max. rate (%)	Avg. rate (%)	Top solv. tax rate (%)	Total tax capacity (%)	TWP	Top schedule Max. rate (%)	Avg. rate (%)	Top solv. tax rate (%)	Total tax capacity (%)
Kentucky	0.443	10.0	5.50		2.44	0.349	10.0	5.50		1.92
Louisiana	0.396	6.0	3.15	0.90	1.60	0.339	6.0	3.15	0.90	1.37
Maine	0.445	6.5	4.45		1.98	0.330	7.5	4.95	0.40	1.77
Maryland	0.373	6.0	4.40		1.64	0.316	8.9	5.45	2.00	2.35
Massachusetts	0.385	7.2	5.10		1.96	0.358	9.3	6.35		2.27
Michigan	0.394	9.0	4.50	1.00	2.17	0.308	9.0	4.65	1.00	1.74
Minnesota	0.471	7.5	4.25	0.60	2.28	0.477	9.0	4.80	0.68	2.61
Mississippi	0.465	6.4	3.25	1.00	1.98	0.365	6.4	3.25		1.19
Missouri	0.406	7.8	3.90	0.90	1.95	0.333	7.8	3.90	0.90	1.60
Montana[a]	0.714	6.4	4.05		2.89	0.686	6.4	4.05		2.78
Nebraska	0.421	5.4	2.75		1.16	0.326	5.4	2.75	0.54	1.07
Nevada[a]	0.590	5.4	3.25		1.92	0.579	5.4	2.83		1.64
New Hampshire	0.408	6.5	4.65	0.50	2.10	0.308	6.5	3.28	0.50	1.16
New Jersey[a]	0.456	6.2	3.70	0.80	2.05	0.458	6.9	4.00	0.35	1.99
New Mexico[a]	0.549	5.4	4.05		2.22	0.541	5.4	4.05		2.19
New York	0.322	6.4	4.25	1.00	1.69	0.213	5.4	3.25	1.20	0.95
North Carolina[a]	0.515	5.7	2.90	0.57	1.79	0.455	5.7	2.85	0.57	1.56

North Dakota[a]	0.567	5.0	2.75		1.56	0.548	5.4	2.95		1.62
Ohio	0.390	5.4	2.80	1.60	1.72	0.334	6.5	3.30	1.28	1.53
Oklahoma[a]	0.462	6.2	3.35	1.15	2.08	0.457	9.2	4.75	1.53	2.87
Oregon[a]	0.629	5.4	3.80		2.39	0.607	5.4	3.80		2.31
Pennsylvania	0.402	9.2	5.35	0.50	2.35	0.297	9.2	5.35	0.80	1.83
Puerto Rico	0.588	5.4	4.18		2.45	0.466	5.4	3.95		1.84
Rhode Island[a]	0.554	8.4	5.35	1.08	3.56	0.556	8.3	5.20	0.30	3.06
South Carolina	0.436	5.4	3.35	0.70	1.77	0.327	5.4	3.32	0.70	1.31
South Dakota	0.465	10.5	6.00	0.80	3.16	0.364	9.5	5.50	0.80	2.29
Tennessee	0.414	10.0	5.25	0.35	2.32	0.306	10.0	5.25		1.61
Texas	0.377	6.0	3.05	1.00	1.53	0.337	6.0	3.00	1.00	1.35
Utah[a]	0.576	8.0	4.15		2.39	0.575	8.0	4.15		2.39
Vermont	0.469	8.4	4.85		2.27	0.351	8.4	4.85		1.70
Virginia	0.392	6.2	3.45	0.20	1.43	0.315	6.4	3.35	0.20	1.12
Virgin Islands[a]	0.778	9.0	4.55	0.75	4.12	0.590	9.0	4.55	0.75	3.13
Washington[a]	0.532	5.4	3.94		2.10	0.584	5.4	3.88		2.27
West Virginia	0.423	7.5	4.50	1.55	2.56	0.357	7.5	4.50		1.61
Wisconsin	0.500	6.7	3.35	0.85	2.10	0.392	8.9	4.59	0.45	1.97
Wyoming[a]	0.508	8.5	4.88		2.48	0.485	8.8	4.55	0.62	2.51
U.S. total	0.408	6.4	3.72	0.64	1.77	0.342	6.8	3.85	0.62	1.53
Indexed states	0.523	6.3	3.75	0.50	2.21	0.519	6.8	3.94	0.35	2.23
Nonindexed states	0.386	6.5	3.72	0.66	1.69	0.306	6.8	3.82	0.68	1.38

SOURCE: U.S. Department of Labor, *Comparison of State Unemployment Insurance Laws.*

[a] State with indexed tax base.

Total tax capacity in 1986 was noticeably higher in states with indexed taxable wage bases. The overall average was 2.21 percent of total wages in indexed states and 1.69 percent in nonindexed states. On average, total tax capacity was about 24 percent lower in nonindexed states. By 1996, the average difference in total tax capacity for indexed and nonindexed states had grown to 38 percent. (The average tax rate was 2.23 percent for indexed states but 1.38 percent for nonindexed states.)

Note also that the average maximum solvency tax had fallen in indexed states but remained essentially unchanged in nonindexed states. In other words, from 1986 to 1996, when the number of indexed and nonindexed states did not change, indexed states maintained their total tax capacity, but nonindexed states did not. The latter were somewhat more exposed to the risks of recession-related indebtedness in 1996 than they had been a decade earlier.

The Distribution of Actual versus Statutory Tax Rates

Since the mid 1980s, UI benefit costs have fallen below long-term averages. From 1986 through 1995, for example, benefits averaged 0.894 percent of covered wages. The average cost rate for the preceding 10 years was 1.197 percent, and for the preceding 40 years (1946 through 1985), 1.128 percent. Thus, from 1986 through 1995, UI costs were about 25 percent below those of the preceding decade and 20 percent below those of the preceding four decades.

The effect of experience-rating during a period of below-average costs should be to reduce average effective tax rates. However, the past decade was also a period when the federal taxable wage base remained at $7,000, and the TWP fell in nearly all nonindexed states. Those states raised revenues from an ever-smaller share of total wages, which undoubtedly acted to restrain reductions in their average tax rates.

Table 3-3 summarizes tax rate developments from 1986–1996. The table shows five data items for both 1986 and 1996: 1) the average statutory tax rate, 2) the average effective tax rate (on taxable wages), 3) the ratio of the average effective tax rate to the average statutory rate, 4) the taxable wage proportion (TWP), and 5) taxes as a percentage of total wages. Each state with an indexed tax base is identified

Table 3-3 Statutory Tax Rates, Effective Tax Rates, and Taxable Wage Proportions, 1986 and 1996

State	1986					1996				
	Avg. stat. rate (%)	Effective tax rate (%)	Effective rate/ stat. rate (%)	TWP	Taxes/total wages (%)	Avg. stat. rate (%)	Effective tax rate (%)	Effective rate/ stat. rate (%)	TWP	Taxes/total wages (%)
Alabama	2.95	2.22	0.753	0.460	1.02	3.73	0.96	0.258	0.352	0.34
Alaska[a]	3.20	2.86	0.894	0.681	1.95	3.75	2.70	0.720	0.654	1.77
Arizona	2.75	1.54	0.560	0.405	0.62	4.15	1.65	0.398	0.316	0.52
Arkansas	3.55	2.37	0.668	0.477	1.13	3.05	1.94	0.636	0.426	0.83
California	2.85	2.34	0.821	0.353	0.83	3.35	3.76	1.122	0.250	0.94
Colorado	2.85	2.08	0.730	0.415	0.86	2.75	1.04	0.378	0.383	0.40
Connecticut	3.95	2.32	0.587	0.324	0.75	4.45	4.04	0.908	0.305	1.23
Delaware	5.55	3.06	0.551	0.402	1.23	4.05	2.42	0.598	0.300	0.73
District of Columbia	4.00	2.97	0.743	0.351	1.04	4.65	2.95	0.634	0.267	0.79
Florida	2.75	1.10	0.400	0.428	0.47	2.75	1.56	0.567	0.319	0.50
Georgia	4.35	1.61	0.370	0.412	0.66	4.08	1.36	0.333	0.331	0.45
Hawaii[a]	2.80	1.68	0.600	0.686	1.15	3.90	2.05	0.526	0.711	1.46
Idaho[a]	3.65	2.98	0.816	0.693	2.07	4.85	1.79	0.369	0.673	1.20
Illinois	4.05	3.99	0.985	0.378	1.51	3.40	2.56	0.753	0.303	0.78
Indiana	2.85	1.44	0.505	0.372	0.54	3.55	1.29	0.363	0.293	0.38
Iowa[a]	4.50	3.19	0.709	0.582	1.86	4.50	0.96	0.213	0.531	0.51
Kansas	3.23	2.00	0.619	0.483	0.97	3.20	0.30	0.094	0.416	0.12
Kentucky	5.50	3.22	0.585	0.443	1.43	5.50	2.06	0.375	0.349	0.72

Table 3-3 (continued)

State	1986					1996				
	Avg. stat. rate (%)	Effective tax rate (%)	Effective rate/ stat. rate (%)	TWP	Taxes/total wages (%)	Avg. stat. rate (%)	Effective tax rate (%)	Effective rate/ stat. rate (%)	TWP	Taxes/total wages (%)
Louisiana	4.30	3.81	0.887	0.396	1.51	3.15	1.69	0.537	0.339	0.57
Maine	3.95	2.70	0.684	0.445	1.20	4.95	3.72	0.752	0.330	1.23
Maryland	3.90	2.76	0.708	0.373	1.03	5.45	2.45	0.450	0.316	0.77
Massachusetts	3.30	2.07	0.627	0.385	0.80	6.35	3.65	0.575	0.358	1.31
Michigan	5.50	5.44	0.989	0.394	2.14	4.65	3.53	0.759	0.308	1.09
Minnesota[a]	4.25	2.71	0.638	0.471	1.28	4.80	1.38	0.288	0.477	0.66
Mississippi	2.95	1.93	0.654	0.465	0.90	3.25	1.32	0.406	0.365	0.48
Missouri	3.90	2.29	0.587	0.406	0.93	3.90	1.99	0.510	0.333	0.66
Montana[a]	4.15	2.30	0.554	0.714	1.64	4.05	1.27	0.314	0.686	0.87
Nebraska	2.75	1.90	0.691	0.421	0.80	2.75	0.92	0.335	0.326	0.30
Nevada[a]	2.85	1.84	0.646	0.590	1.09	2.83	1.54	0.545	0.579	0.89
New Hampshire	3.26	0.82	0.252	0.408	0.33	3.28	1.01	0.308	0.308	0.31
New Jersey[a]	4.05	2.98	0.736	0.456	1.36	4.00	2.53	0.633	0.458	1.16
New Mexico[a]	3.15	1.98	0.629	0.549	1.09	4.05	1.33	0.328	0.541	0.72
New York	3.85	3.25	0.844	0.322	1.05	3.25	4.41	1.357	0.213	0.94
North Carolina[a]	3.48	1.85	0.532	0.515	0.95	2.85	0.22	0.077	0.455	0.10
North Dakota[a]	3.85	2.86	0.743	0.567	1.62	2.95	0.83	0.281	0.548	0.45

Ohio	4.40	3.61	0.820	0.390	1.41	3.30	2.27	0.688	0.334	0.76
Oklahoma[a]	4.75	2.34	0.493	0.462	1.08	4.75	0.87	0.183	0.457	0.40
Oregon[a]	3.80	3.11	0.818	0.629	1.96	3.80	2.10	0.553	0.607	1.27
Pennsylvania	6.15	5.03	0.818	0.402	2.02	5.35	4.26	0.796	0.297	1.27
Puerto Rico	4.18	5.34	1.279	0.588	3.14	3.95	3.34	0.846	0.466	1.56
Rhode Island[a]	5.35	3.73	0.697	0.554	2.07	5.20	3.68	0.708	0.556	2.05
South Carolina	3.35	2.01	0.600	0.436	0.88	3.32	1.90	0.572	0.327	0.62
South Dakota	4.55	1.44	0.316	0.465	0.67	5.50	0.55	0.100	0.364	0.20
Tennessee	5.08	1.72	0.339	0.414	0.71	5.25	1.63	0.310	0.306	0.50
Texas	4.36	2.04	0.468	0.377	0.77	3.00	1.53	0.510	0.337	0.52
Utah[a]	4.15	1.80	0.434	0.576	1.04	4.15	0.87	0.210	0.575	0.50
Vermont	4.85	3.98	0.821	0.469	1.87	4.85	2.60	0.536	0.351	0.91
Virginia	4.55	1.29	0.284	0.392	0.51	3.35	1.16	0.346	0.315	0.37
Virgin Islands[a]	3.15	3.44	1.092	0.778	2.68	4.55	2.83	0.622	0.590	1.67
Washington[a]	3.94	4.03	1.023	0.532	2.14	3.88	1.88	0.485	0.584	1.10
West Virginia	6.00	4.52	0.753	0.423	1.91	4.50	2.97	0.660	0.357	1.06
Wisconsin	5.20	4.62	0.888	0.500	2.31	4.59	2.02	0.441	0.392	0.79
Wyoming[a]	5.00	3.40	0.680	0.508	1.73	4.55	1.49	0.327	0.485	0.72
U.S. total	3.96	2.77	0.700	0.408	1.13	3.85	2.28	0.592	0.342	0.78
Indexed states	3.94	2.74	0.696	0.523	1.43	3.94	1.60	0.405	0.519	0.83
Nonindexed states	3.97	2.78	0.701	0.386	1.08	3.82	2.51	0.657	0.306	0.77

SOURCE: U.S. Department of Labor, *Comparison of State Unemployment Insurance Laws*.
[a] State with indexed tax base.

and overall averages are shown for both indexed and nonindexed states.

Two comments are needed. First, the average statutory rate is measured as the simple average of the minimum and maximum rates for the year and includes solvency taxes if they were activated. Second, the ratio of the average effective rate to the average statutory rate is not constrained to fall below unity. The ratio shows where the central tendency of the actual tax rate distribution falls relative to the center of the statutory tax rate schedule. As the distribution of actual rates moves downward towards the minimum rate, this ratio will decrease.

Three contrasting patterns for indexed and nonindexed states are apparent in Table 3-3. First, the overall averages for the statutory rates, the effective tax rates, and the ratio of the effective rates to statutory rates were quite similar in 1986; the latter ratios were 0.696 and 0.701 for indexed and nonindexed states, respectively. However, because the TWP was systematically higher for the indexed states in 1986 (0.523 versus 0.386), taxes as a percent of total wages were considerably higher in the indexed states (1.43 percent versus 1.08 percent).

Second, the average statutory rate did not change much in either the indexed (unchanged at 3.94 in both years) or the nonindexed states (decreasing from 3.97 to 3.82 percent). However, during the same period, the effective tax rate for indexed states dropped sharply (from 2.74 to 1.60, or by 42 percent), while the decrease was much smaller in nonindexed states (from 2.78 to 2.51, or by 10 percent). As a result, the decline in the ratio of effective tax rates to statutory tax rates in indexed states was 42 percent (from 0.696 to 0.405), while in nonindexed states it was only 6 percent (from 0.701 to 0.657). The effective tax rate distribution moved significantly towards the minimum rate in the indexed states, while it was little changed in nonindexed states. On average, employers in indexed states were being taxed at much lower rates along their tax schedules in 1996 than were employers in nonindexed states.

Third, as noted previously, the average TWP was roughly stable in the indexed states, while it fell by 20 percent in nonindexed states (from 0.386 to 0.306). Because the TWP was so much higher in indexed states, average taxes on total wages were higher in those states (0.83 percent) than in nonindexed states (0.77 percent). This represents a much smaller average effective tax rate differential than in

1986. The key difference between the indexed and nonindexed states in 1996 was that indexed states had a much higher capacity for increasing revenues. That increase could be accomplished within their experience-rating systems, which allowed a greater range for moving the average effective tax rate towards the maximum statutory rate (as reflected by the lower ratio of the average effective tax rate to the average statutory rate in indexed states). As shown in Table 2-5, the tax capacity for experience-rated taxes in indexed states was much greater than that tax capacity in nonindexed states in 1996 (2.05 percent versus 1.17 percent of total wages).

Maintaining Reserves in the Long Run

In assessing the impact of indexing on UI financing, it is important to move beyond the focus on tax rates in Table 3-3. A state's ability to build and maintain adequate reserves is the main indicator of successful program funding.

The reserve ratio multiples for individual states in 1989 and 1996 are shown in Table 1-4 of Chapter 1. Weighted averages of those multiples for 1989 and 1996 were computed for indexed and nonindexed UI programs. The 1989 and 1996 national averages for those multiples were 0.87 and 0.64, respectively. The corresponding averages for indexed states in 1989 and 1996 were 1.18 and 0.88, each about one-third above the national average. For nonindexed states, the corresponding averages were 0.81 and 0.59, respectively. As indicators of reserve adequacy, these multiples show that indexed programs were more adequately financed than nonindexed programs in both years.

When the individual RRMs are examined for the 18 programs with indexed tax base, the expected patterns emerge. None of the 10 programs with the lowest multiples in 1989 had an indexed tax base. In 1996, only one of the bottom 10 (Rhode Island) had an indexed tax base. Of the top 10 multiples in 1989 and 1996, numbers five and six were from programs with indexed tax bases.[7] When states were ranked from bottom to top, the average rankings for indexed programs in 1989 and 1996 were 34.3 and 32.6, respectively, while the corresponding averages for nonindexed programs were 21.7 and 22.6, respectively. The high average multiples for indexed states reflect a generalized pattern, not just the effects of high multiples in a few programs with indexed tax bases.

As noted, reserve ratio multiples declined generally between 1989 and 1996, for both indexed and nonindexed programs. However, because indexed programs had higher multiples in 1989, the declines for those programs had less serious implications for future borrowing and indebtedness.

A cautionary comment about interpreting the differences in the average reserve positions: some states may be more proactive in accumulating substantial reserves (placing greater emphasis on advance funding as opposed to pay-as-you-go). These states may also be proactive in a second area, that is, in instituting and maintaining an indexed tax base. With indexing, however, the need for other proactive measures for maintaining large balances is reduced, for the tax base automatically grows with average wages in the state.

Distinguishing between a proactive public policy that leads to larger trust fund reserves and indexed taxes bases that also lead to larger reserves might not be easy, but that indexed states have higher reserve ratio multiples is clear. In both 1989 and 1996, the average reserve ratio multiple for indexed states was almost 50 percent above the average multiple for the nonindexed states.[8]

Maintaining Reserves During Recessions

An indexed tax base can help states compensate for recession-related losses in reserves. The automatic growth in taxable wages per employee helps to offset the revenue losses caused by the lower levels of employment.

Appendix B reports the results of a regression analysis of the effect of indexing on trust fund reserves. The analysis examines recession-related drawdowns for 1974–1976, 1981–1983, and 1990–1992. Multiple regressions were fitted for each period to test for the partial effect of tax-base indexing on the size of trust fund drawdowns.

The results support the hypothesis that tax-base indexing has a positive effect on trust fund reserves during recessions. States with indexed tax bases (identified with dummy variables) had significantly smaller losses in reserves for each of the three recessions. The size of the dummy variable coefficients, 0.16 to 0.54 in 10 of 12 regressions, suggests that the effects of tax-base indexing are significant.

Nonetheless, caution is advised in interpreting these results. States with indexed tax bases may generally be taking a proactive approach to trust fund management and may want to maintain large reserves. Thus, from a more general perspective, the underlying cause may be that a proactive policy leads to larger trust fund balances, and tax-base indexing may also serve to indicate a proactive approach to trust fund management.

SUMMARY

Tax-base indexing has been consistently used in 18 UI programs since 1986. Those programs have significantly higher tax bases and much higher taxable wage proportions when compared with other UI programs. The indexed programs maintained their average taxable wage proportions during 1986–1996, but those proportions dropped markedly in nonindexed programs.

From the comparative analysis of indexed and nonindexed states come three conclusions:

1. UI programs with indexed tax bases were more successful than nonindexed ones in maintaining their tax capacity (potential taxes as a percentage of total covered wages). The differences in average tax capacity for indexed and nonindexed programs (as measured in Table 3-2) grew from 24 percent in 1986 to 38 percent in 1996.

2. Tax-base indexing is associated with higher trust fund reserves, as measured by reserve ratio multiples. In both 1989 and 1996, the average RRM was about 50 percent higher in indexed than in nonindexed states.

3. A regression analysis found that tax-base indexing significantly helped states maintain trust fund reserves during recessions. Clearly, tax-base indexing offers both short- and long-term advantages in maintaining trust fund reserves.

Notes

1. Respectively, the TWP increased by 0.002, 0.017, 0.001, and 0.003 in those four years.
2. It should also be noted that average wages grew very slowly, less than 2.2 percent, during both 1993 and 1994.
3. Some states with indexed maximum WBAs have frozen those provisions to prevent insolvency. Of the even-numbered years between 1986 and 1996, the year with the highest incidence of such limitations was 1988, when 10 states overrode the indexing provision of their maximum WBA.
4. California and Texas accounted for 46 percent of covered employment in the West in 1995.
5. Puerto Rico, a low-wage jurisdiction with a 1996 tax base of $7,000, ranked 16th.
6. Seven states use array allocations: Alaska, Idaho, Iowa, Kansas, North Dakota, Vermont, and Washington. All but Washington have employment levels below the national average.
7. States were assigned numbers from 1 (the lowest reserve ratio multiple) to 53 (the highest multiple). Simple averages of the ranks were then computed for the 19 indexed and for the 35 nonindexed programs.
8. In 1989, the reserve ratio multiple for indexed states averaged 1.180, while in nonindexed states the multiple averaged 0.807. The corresponding average multiples in 1996 were 0.883 and 0.591, respectively.

4 Financing Unemployment Insurance Debts

This chapter examines methods of financing state UI trust fund indebtedness.[1] The two main options are the traditional method—borrowing from the U.S. Treasury—and a recent innovation, the direct issuing of bonds by debtor states. The chapter describes the two options, assesses their strengths and weaknesses, reviews the history of state borrowing and bond issuing, and compares costs.

It is important to state at the outset that, as in many other public policy debates, there is no single answer about whether it is better to issue state debt instruments than to borrow from the U.S. Treasury. The specific circumstances of a debtor state need to be assessed, and the issuing of state debt itself entails a number of options. The question is thus not either/or, but rather one that considers a number of alternatives in issuing state debt.

BACKGROUND

The recession of the early 1990s was mild by history's standards, both in terms of the peak-to-trough decline in real output and in the level of overall joblessness. The unemployment rate peaked at 7.7 percent of the civilian labor force in June 1992 and fell steadily after that date. The annual average unemployment rate fell from 7.5 percent in 1992 to 5.4 percent in 1996 and reached even lower levels in early 1997.

Because state UI trust funds had grown substantially between 1984 and 1989, and because the recession was comparatively mild, state trust fund reserves were generally high enough to meet the increased demand for benefits during the recession of the 1990s. Only seven UI programs needed loans from the U.S. Treasury, and only Connecticut and Massachusetts experienced substantial indebtedness. Connecticut and Massachusetts borrowed in 1991, the District of Columbia and Michigan in 1992, and Maine, Missouri, and New York in 1993. All loans were fully repaid by June 1995. Borrowing during 1991–1995 totaled $4.8 billion, with Connecticut ($1.66 billion) and Massachusetts ($1.72 billion) accounting for 70 percent of the national total. The experience of the 1990s contrasts sharply with that of the mid 1970s and of the early 1980s. Between 1980 and 1987, 32 UI programs borrowed a total of $24.2 billion.

Traditionally, UI trust fund debts have been financed by loans from the U.S. Treasury. After these loans started to carry interest charges in the early 1980s, states began to repay their loans much more rapidly.[2] This pattern of rapid loan repayment continued in the 1990s. During 1991 and 1992, for example, $2.2 billion was borrowed, but $1.4 billion was repaid.

Another change in debt repayment dating from the 1980s was direct bond issuing by debtor states to repay their U.S. Treasury loans. Louisiana and West Virginia issued tax-free bonds for that purpose. Those bonds were later retired using the proceeds of state payroll taxes.

Several states explored state bond financing during the recession of the early 1990s. Connecticut, Massachusetts, Michigan, and Maine held discussions with potential underwriters. The lower interest rates associated with tax-free bonds was a major point of emphasis in those discussions. In June 1993, Connecticut authorized a bond issue of about $1.0 billion as one element of its UI solvency legislation. Massachusetts considered a bond package during its 1992 legislative session but did not enact it.

Because state bond issues will undoubtedly be considered in future recessions, the following analysis may be useful to states considering issuing bonds.

FINANCING WITH U.S. TREASURY LOANS

Title XII of the Social Security Act sets the legal requirements that states must satisfy when borrowing to finance UI trust fund debts. Essentially, loans are available on an "as needed" basis, with interest charges accruing if advances still remain outstanding after certain dates. Repayment of the principal can be made on a voluntary basis, but if a minimum rate of repayment is not achieved, automatic repayment is accomplished through special taxes added to each employer's federal UI tax.

Several legal requirements are imposed on debtor states by Title XII, by other parts of the Social Security Act, and by the Federal Unemployment Tax Act. A useful starting point is to look at the trust fund withdrawal standard. Each state maintains a trust fund account at the U.S. Treasury. Inflows come from two sources: state UI taxes and interest earnings on account balances that are invested in specialized U.S. Treasury debt instruments. Outflows are reserved for a single purpose: to pay benefits to UI claimants.[3]

The withdrawal standard and associated regulations limits the choices available to a debtor state. Monies in the state trust fund accounts cannot be used to pay interest on outstanding debts.[4] Also, although the proceeds of a bond issue can be used to repay outstanding Title XII debts, they cannot be deposited into a state's UI trust fund account in anticipation of future debts. In other words, a debtor state owing $500 million on September 30th but expecting to borrow another $100 million during October–December can deposit only $500 million from a bond issue on September 30th. Additional proceeds from a bond issue can be deposited only as new trust fund debts accrue.

Interest charges on Title XII debt are calculated as the product of average daily indebtedness times the interest rate on long-term U.S. Treasury debt. The average daily balance is a simple average of indebtedness at the end of each business day in the year. Debtor states can minimize that balance by following a daily debt management strategy. The optimal strategy is to borrow each day that withdrawals exceed receipts and repay on days that receipts exceed withdrawals. The strategy minimizes the average daily balance and leaves the fund balance at zero at the end of each day. The interest rate charged on debt is the average interest rate earned by states with positive UI trust fund balances during the fourth quarter of the previous calendar year and is subject to a maximum rate of 10.0 percent.[5]

States that borrow after January 1st of a given year can avoid interest charges altogether if the loans are fully repaid by September 30th, the last day of the fiscal year. Loans taken and fully repaid within a fiscal year are commonly referred to as "cash-flow" loans. If, however, there is additional borrowing between October 1st and December 31st, the state is then subject to full interest charges on the earlier borrowing[6] as well as interest on the October–December borrowing.

Interest payments on loans for a given fiscal year are due on September 30th, but interest payments for loans received after April 30th can be deferred until December 31st of the following year. Additional interest continues to accrue, adding to the state's interest liability; for example, under an annual interest rate of 10.0 percent, a state that borrowed during May–September and owed $12 million in interest on September 30th would owe $13.5 million if it deferred all repayments until December 31 of the following year.

States also need to consider monthly patterns of trust fund receipts and expenditures. Benefit payments in most states exhibit a pronounced seasonal pattern because the average number of beneficiaries during January and February is typically much larger than during July and August. The normal seasonal variation in claims can cause January and February benefit payments to be 40 to 50 percent higher than July and August payments.

Trust fund tax receipts are also highly seasonal, but their month-to-month patterns are much more irregular than those of benefit payments. Employers' tax obligations accrue in each quarter, with payments usually due early in the following quarter.[7] Thus, tax receipts are heavily concentrated in February, May, August, and November. Also, because of the low taxable wage base, receipts in May (based on first-quarter taxable wages) are by far the largest, followed in descending order by receipts in August, November, and February of the next year. In states with tax bases close to the federal tax base of $7,000 per worker, receipts in May can be four to eight times the receipts of the following February.

These seasonal patterns are generally predictable, even though tax receipts and benefit outlays can both be quite volatile in the short run. Since the patterns of receipts and outlays are so different, a debtor state will typically make substantial loan repayments in some months and borrow large amounts in others. Borrowing during January and repaying during May are to be expected, even for a state whose annual receipts fall substantially short of its annual withdrawals.

The experiences of Massachusetts and Connecticut during 1991 and 1992 vividly illustrate this point.[8] Connecticut started borrowing in January 1991, and Massachusetts secured its first loan in August

1991. During 1991 and 1992, benefit outlays substantially exceeded tax revenues in both states. Connecticut's year-end debt totaled $354 million in 1991 and $653 million in 1992; the corresponding levels for Massachusetts were $234 million and $380 million. Yet, both states made sizeable loan repayments during the two years. Connecticut, which had the more serious funding imbalance,[9] repaid $148 million in 1991 and $202 million in 1992, while borrowing about $500 million in each year. Massachusetts borrowed $732 million in 1992, while repaying $589 million. In both states, loan repayments were concentrated in months of high tax receipts. However, because receipts arrive irregularly during the month, borrowing occurred even in these months.

To summarize, after a state exhausts its trust fund and starts to borrow, it typically borrows in every month and makes loan repayments in at least four months, for example, in February, May, August, and November. This pattern of borrowing and repaying is rational, because it minimizes the average daily level of debt.

Connecticut and Massachusetts addressed their funding problems through legislation. In January 1992, the taxable wage base in Massachusetts increased from $7,000 to $10,800, and new tax rate schedules came into effect. Tax receipts in May 1992 reflected the effects of Massachusetts' higher tax base and higher scheduled tax rates. Large loan repayments occurred during May 1992 ($319 million) and May 1993 ($334 million). A repayment of $257 million in May 1994 fully eliminated the debt.

Connecticut, on the other hand, had a serious funding imbalance which it did not address until June 1993. Its 1993 legislation raised the taxable wage base (to $9,000 in 1994 and eventually to $15,000 in 1999), increased the maximum solvency tax (from 1.0 percent to 1.5 percent), and made modest benefit reductions. It also authorized borrowing through a state bond issue. Roughly $1.0 billion in state bonds was issued during August–September 1993, both to repay its outstanding Title XII loans and to cover possible later borrowing. This bond issue is discussed below.

Title XII also specifies debt repayment requirements. As noted, for any period when receipts exceed outlays, the excess can be used to retire the outstanding debt instead of remaining in the state's trust fund account. If debt has been outstanding on January 1st of two consecutive years and has not been fully repaid by November 10th of the later year, automatic repayment begins. On January 1st of the following year, 0.3 percent is added to the federal part of the tax obligation (the FUTA tax) for each covered employer in the state. In other words, the rate rises from 0.8 to 1.1 percent of federal taxable wages (the first $7,000 of annual earnings).[10] The proceeds of this "penalty tax"[11] go to repay the oldest portion of the state's outstanding debt.

If a state continues to carry outstanding debt, additional FUTA penalty taxes are imposed in subsequent years. The proceeds are used to retire debt, always starting with the oldest remaining debt. The rate of the penalty tax increases in the second and subsequent later years.[12] Thus, if a state does not take steps to repay its debt, an automatic mechanism will eventually bring about full repayment.

FUTA penalty taxes for each year are imposed at a single flat rate on all covered employers. A state may prefer to make loan repayments by using taxes for which rates vary across employers. To do this, it may either divert part of its regular tax receipts into voluntary repayments (if receipts exceed outlays by a sufficient margin) or impose additional taxes (as a fixed proportion of regular state UI taxes). Voluntary repayments of either kind may be made in lieu of mandatory FUTA penalty taxes, but they must at least equal the yield of the FUTA penalty tax.

STATE BOND ISSUES

Another method for financing UI debts is to issue state-backed debt instruments, with the proceeds primarily going to repay outstanding Title XII loans. State debt instruments are free from federal income tax, so the interest rate on state instruments is usually much lower than on Title XII loans. Debt repayment takes place in later years, typically using the proceeds of a separate payroll tax on UI covered employment.[13]

State debt issues are usefully seen as a generic alternative to Title XII borrowing. There are, however, many variations. Louisiana and West Virginia issued state debt in 1987 and Connecticut in August–September 1993. Those issues covered only part of the range of potential borrowing arrangements. States must decide the volume of needed borrowing, the breakdown between immediate and anticipated needs, the maturity structure, and the source of repayment. Arrangements that are appropriate for one state may not be appropriate for another.

In deciding whether to issue its debt, a state will be influenced by the costs of different borrowing arrangements. Cost comparisons must consider both the future interest rate spreads between Title XII loans and state debt and the costs of issuing state debt. Moreover, once a state issues its debt, there can be no forgiveness of interest costs (unlike Title XII loans fully repaid by September 30th). Finally, there are questions about the appropriate, or optimal, lag between the date that the need for borrowing is recognized and the date that the debt should be issued.

Proponents of state debt issues note that interest rates on state bonds are typically at least 100 basis points lower than interest rates on long-term U.S. bonds.[14] Table 4-1 provides summary data for selected short- and long-term interest rates from 1975 to 1996. It also shows differences in interest rates, or spreads, for these years. The table begins with 1975 because that was the first year of substantial Title XII borrowing during the 1970s. Even though loans were interest-free until 1982, covering a longer period provides a more complete picture of the variability in interest rates and of the spreads between selected pairs of interest rates. The table gives the interest rates for Title XII loans,[15] the rates for Aaa municipal bonds, and two short-term rates.

Aaa municipal bonds are the highest-grade state and local government long-term debt instruments. They carry lower interest rates than bonds in higher risk categories (such as Aa, A, and Baa). From 1975 through 1996, the average spread between the rates on Aaa bonds and A bonds, for example, was 48 basis points. The ratings to be expected for UI-related debt would generally be in the Aaa to A range. A lower-risk (and thus a higher-rated) issue would be expected if the bonds were insured or supported by a bank letter of credit, and if the state's overall finances were judged to be strong. Another factor influencing the rating for a state's debt issue is whether the state's regular method of collecting its UI taxes can also be used to collect the state taxes designed to repay the principal of a bond issue.

In each year from 1985 to 1996, the Title XII rate exceeded the Aaa municipal bond rate by more than 100 basis points. During that

Table 4-1 Selected Interest Rates and Interest Rate Spreads, 1975–1996[a]

	Interest rates:				Basis point spreads:				
Year	Title XII loans	Moody Aaa munic. bonds	6 mo. taxable comm. paper	1 mo. tax-free comm. paper	Title XII less bonds	Title XI less taxable comm. paper	Title XII less tax-free comm. paper	Bonds less taxable comm. paper	Bonds less tax-free comm. paper
1975	5.92	6.42	6.32	NA[b]	-50	-40	NA	10	NA
1976	4.68	5.66	5.34	NA	-98	-66	NA	32	NA
1977	5.26	5.20	5.61	NA	6	-35	NA	-41	NA
1978	5.56	5.52	7.99	NA	4	-243	NA	-247	NA
1979	6.25	5.92	10.91	NA	33	-466	NA	-499	NA
1980	7.17	7.85	12.29	NA	-68	-512	NA	-444	NA
1981	8.80	10.43	14.76	NA	-163	-596	NA	-433	NA
1982	10.00	11.33	11.89	NA	-133	-189	NA	-56	NA
1983	10.00	8.80	8.89	NA	120	111	NA	-9	NA
1984	9.78	9.51	10.16	NA	27	-38	NA	-65	NA
1985	10.00	8.60	8.01	NA	140	199	NA	59	NA
1986	9.96	6.95	6.39	4.25	301	357	571	56	270
1987	9.33	7.14	6.85	4.45	219	248	488	29	269
1988	8.54	7.35	7.68	5.28	119	86	326	-33	207
1989	8.33	6.99	8.80	6.23	134	-47	210	-181	76

1990	8.70	6.96	7.95	5.77	174	75	293	-99	119
1991	8.60	6.56	5.85	4.21	204	275	439	71	235
1992	8.05	6.09	3.80	2.62	196	425	543	229	347
1993	7.45	5.38	3.30	2.19	207	415	526	208	319
1994	6.90	5.77	4.93	2.60	113	197	430	84	317
1995	6.83	5.80	5.93	3.62	103	90	321	-13	218
1996	6.71	5.52	5.42	3.19	119	129	352	10	233

SOURCE: Table B–71 of the Economic Report of the President, January 1997; the UI Service; and Goldman, Sachs and Co.

[a] All data are annual averages. There are 100 basis points in each percentage point of an interest rate.

[b] NA = data could not be obtained for 1975–1986.

time, the spread ranged from 103 basis points (1995) to 301 basis points (1986) and averaged 169 basis points.

Note that the spreads between Title XII and Aaa interest rates spreads were much smaller before 1985 and that the Aaa rate exceeded the Title XII rate in five of the earlier years. The average Aaa rate was actually higher by 32 basis points from 1975 through 1984 (7.66 percent versus 7.34 percent). In years of high interest rates like 1980–1985, the 10.0 percent ceiling on Title XII loans is an important consideration.

Assessing future interest rate spreads between Title XII loans and Aaa municipal bonds involves a number of uncertainties. From the data shown in Table 4-1 ("Title XII less bonds" column), it is clear that spreads in favor of Aaa municipal bonds were especially large in 1986 and 1987 and again in 1990 through 1993.

However, there are several other factors to keep in mind when evaluating future interest rate differentials. First, spreads between short- and long-term interest rates can also be large, such as during the early 1990s. Both short-term rates were less than 4.0 percent in 1992 and 1993, and neither exceeded 6.0 percent between 1993 and 1996. Note that the interest rate for one-month tax-free commercial paper is consistently the lowest short-term rate (Table 4-1). That rate was more than 200 basis points below the rate for Aaa municipal bonds for every year between 1991 and 1996. States with short-term and intermediate-term needs can take advantage of very low short-term interest rates. Second, states needing to finance UI debts during the 1980s and the 1990s typically paid off their debts quite rapidly.[16] Clearly, the need for long-term financing must be carefully evaluated. Issuing debt instruments with, say, 10-year maturities would not be prudent if state indebtedness were to last only two or three years. Third, a comparison of the costs of state bond issues and Title XII loans must factor in the costs of underwriting fees (commissions and insurance) along with interest rate spreads.

A state that issues its own debt instruments would be motivated primarily by the prospect of reducing its debt-related interest costs.[17] Key to a state's deliberations are its expectations about the time-pattern of its borrowing as well as Title XII loan repayment rules. Finally, since spreads between short- and long-term rates can be large, the cost advantages of short-term debt issues also need to be considered.

The following strategy could prove very useful for a state that is starting to need loans:

- Borrow and repay Title XII loans on a daily basis.

- Pay off all outstanding Title XII loans obtained between January 1st and September 30th by issuing tax-free commercial paper on September 30th.

- Issue additional paper as needed during the period from October 1st to December 31st. (At 1996 interest rates, the annual rate of interest on such borrowing would be about 3.2 percent, about 230 basis points lower than the 1996 Aaa municipal bond rate of 5.52 percent.)

- As short-term debts mature, consolidate the borrowing into tax-free six-month commercial paper.

The strategy takes advantage of both the interest-free feature of Title XII loans in the first year of the debt and the interest rate spread favoring short rates in the first and subsequent years (for as long as short-term rates are considerably lower than long-term rates). The costs of the issue need to be factored into the calculations, but they are comparatively modest for short-term commercial paper. Brokerage fees and insurance combined would probably add less than 50 basis points to the annual interest rate. In other words, the issue and re-issue of six-month tax-free commercial paper would have an annual cost (including underwriting fees) of 4.0 to 4.5 percent at 1996 interest rates.

In structuring a debt-issuing strategy, a state needs to consider general obligation bonds, revenue bonds, fixed maturity bonds, callable bonds, notes and commercial paper.[18] All are free from federal income taxes when issued by states. States can achieve flexibility in repaying their debt by issuing short-term instruments (commercial paper and notes) and/or by having a portion of the long-term debt (bonds) be callable.

The underwriting fees (commissions plus insurance) associated with various debt instruments are roughly as follows (all measured at annual rates): fixed bonds and callable bonds with 10-year maturities, 80 to 100 basis points; three-year notes, 50 to 60 basis points; and commercial paper, 35 to 50 basis points.[19] Typically, interest rates are higher for callable bonds than for fixed maturity bonds (30–50 basis points) and higher for revenue bonds than for general obligation bonds.

To achieve flexibility and minimize costs, it would seem that a state should issue a mixed portfolio of debt instruments. States with substantial debts (for example, Connecticut in early 1993), would probably need different portfolios than states just starting to borrow. Whether a state is likely to enact solvency legislation to improve the balance between its revenues and benefit payments is also important.[20] Finally, the spread of interest rates by maturity that favored short-term debt issues in 1992 and 1993 cannot necessarily be expected in the future. The "best" package would depend heavily on the structure of interest rates at the time of the issue.

STATE EXPERIENCES WITH BOND ISSUES

During the mid 1970s and the early to mid 1980s, many UI programs received Title XII loans. Between 1980 and 1988, state borrowing totaled $24.2 billion, of which $19.4 billion secured after April 1, 1982, was interest-bearing.

As noted, repayment patterns changed sharply in 1982 after new loans started to carry interest charges.[21] For each year between 1984 and 1988, annual loan repayment rates (repayments as a fraction of new loans plus interest-bearing debt at the start of the year) exceeded 0.50. Rapid repayments also occurred for loans secured during the 1990s.

After emerging from the back-to-back recessions of the early 1980s, most states experienced a long and sustained economic recovery that lasted through 1988 or 1989. However, states dependent on energy extraction (petroleum and coal) suffered another downturn in the mid 1980s. The unemployment rate in Texas, for example, increased from 5.9 percent of the labor force in 1984 to 8.9 percent in 1986 and remained substantially above the national average through 1989.

Three states still having interest-bearing debts at the end of 1986 were energy producers: Louisiana, Texas, and West Virginia. All three strongly considered issuing state bonds to repay their Title XII loans, and Louisiana and West Virginia did issue bonds in 1987. The third state to issue bonds was Connecticut, which did so in 1993. Louisiana and West Virginia have fully paid off their bonds. An analysis of the comparative costs of bond issues versus the use of Title XII loans is undertaken later in this chapter.

Both Louisiana and West Virginia had very high unemployment in the early 1980s and then a second downturn associated with the energy glut of 1985-1986.[22] Following the 1985–1986 downturn, both states issued municipal bonds to fully repay their Title XII advances in 1987. The bonds were subsequently repaid by payroll taxes on UI-covered employers in Louisiana and by payroll taxes on both employers and workers in West Virginia. West Virginia completed its repayments in 1991 (two years earlier than initially anticipated), and Louisiana completed its bond repayments during 1993.

Table 4-2 shows the summary data for Louisiana for 1979 to 1994. Note how benefit payments increased sharply to $482 million and $596 million in 1982 and 1983, respectively. The state's net trust fund balance dropped from $210 million at the end of 1981 to –$476 million two years later. Borrowing during 1983 alone totaled $427 million. Although taxes increased following the 1982–1983 trust fund drawdown, they remained below benefit outlays until 1988. There was not a single year between 1980 and 1987 that taxes exceeded benefit payments.[23]

Because unemployment and benefit outlays remained high after 1983, Louisiana did not make substantial inroads into its debt. In fact, its net indebtedness continued to rise during 1984 and 1985. High unemployment remained a problem and unemployment rose again during the energy crisis of 1985. The annual unemployment rate for the civilian labor force age 16 and older, which never fell below 10.0 percent between 1982 and 1988, rose during 1985 and 1986 and peaked at 13.1 percent in 1986. Benefit outlays also rose during 1985 and 1986, and Louisiana's borrowing during 1986 totaled $423 million, nearly equaling its borrowing during 1983.

Louisiana's bond issue of 1987 fully repaid its outstanding Title XII loans. Since 1987, the state has gradually rebuilt its trust fund. Fund accumulations were rapid from 1993 through 1996, reaching $869 million at the end of 1994 and $1,131 million at the end of 1996

112

Table 4-2 Summary of Louisiana's UI Trust Fund Activities, 1979 to 1994[a] ($ millions)

	UI trust fund flows			UI trust fund reserves			Title XII loans			State bonds	
Year	Taxes	Interest	Benefits	Gross reserves	Net reserves	U.S. Treasury debt	Loans	Repayments	Debt	Scheduled repayments	Bond taxes
1979	250	12	140	238	238	0	0	0	0	NA[b]	NA
1980	178	20	208	223	223	0	0	0	0	NA	NA
1981	192	21	227	210	210	0	0	0	0	NA	NA
1982	182	6	482	0	-102	102	102	0	102	NA	NA
1983	288	0	596	0	-476	476	427	53	476	NA	NA
1984	357	0	397	0	-521	521	132	88	521	NA	NA
1985	362	0	446	0	-577	577	252	196	577	NA	NA
1986	315	0	538	0	-787	787	423	213	787	NA	NA
1987	306	0	355	1	1	0	184	971	0	0	130
1988	315	7	205	154	154	0	0	0	0	49	192
1989	285	20	151	306	306	0	0	0	0	56	197
1990	236	34	120	456	456	0	0	0	0	59	207
1991	216	43	158	560	560	0	0	0	0	63	211
1992	200	45	204	601	601	0	0	0	0	67	209
1993	193	46	158	689	689	0	0	0	0	72	212
1994	208	54	145	869	869	0	0	0	0	77	0
1995–2002										872	

SOURCE: Data on trust fund transactions including Title XII activities from the U.S. Department of Labor. Data on the scheduled repayment of the state bonds is from the state of Louisiana. Estimates of state bond taxes are made by the author.
[a] Reserves and debt are measured at the year end.
[b] NA = not applicable, as state bonds were issued in 1987.

(see Table 1-4). Louisiana's trust fund balance, however, did not reach a reserve ratio multiple of 1.0 until the end of 1995.

Louisiana issued $1,315 million in serial revenue bonds in September 1987, with maturities in each year from 1988 through 2002. The issue consisted of $921 million of fixed maturity bonds (with due dates from 1988 through 1999) and $394 million of callable bonds (with due dates from 2000 through 2002). Even the fixed maturity part of the issue had call options that could be exercised as early as 1994 for bonds with later maturities.

To finance the bond issue, Louisiana levied a flat-rate employer payroll tax of 1.4 percent on each employee's annual earnings, up to a maximum of $15,000 for each year between 1988 and 1993.[24] The tax, called a "special assessment for debt service," generated about $200 million in annual revenues from 1988 through 1993.

Tax collection and debt management services were performed by a trustee bank. There were three main trust accounts: a benefit transfer account (originally established to cover possible additional borrowing), a reserve fund (mainly a hedge against unexpected tax shortfalls), and an interest fund. At the time of the initial issue, $780 million was used immediately to repay Title XII loans. The rest of the $1,315 million was used to defray issue costs or was deposited into the trust accounts.[25] The three trust accounts were managed with the objective of paying off the bonds as soon as possible so that the special employer tax assessment could be discontinued. To cover the costs of collecting the special assessment tax, the trustee transferred $250,000 to the Louisiana Department of Labor each year.

Louisiana discontinued its special tax assessment after 1993. By that year, its bond liabilities were fully covered. Repayment of the bonds was accomplished by retiring the serial bonds, exercising options on the callable bonds, and establishing an escrow account for serial bonds that became callable in September 1994. Repayment of callable bonds was completed in 1994.

To summarize, Louisiana repaid its Title XII loans with a bond issue in 1987. The total transferred to the state's UI trust fund account was approximately $820 million. Louisiana borrowed a total of $1,315 million in the bond market, with bond maturities spread from 1988 through 2002. In fact, all bond obligations were met in 1993, nine years before the last of the original maturity dates. Debt repayments were completed in 1994.

Table 4-3 gives summary data for West Virginia's trust fund from 1979 to 1994. The state began with low reserves at the end of 1979 ($39 million), first borrowed in 1980, and did so in every subsequent year through 1987. The maximum borrowing, $152 million in 1983, coincided with the high benefit outlays of the 1982–1983 recession.

In the three years after 1983, the state's net reserve position improved somewhat. However, net reserves were still negative, –$225 million, at the end of 1986, a three-year improvement of only $62 million. The time series of taxes and benefits in Table 4-3 shows that both remained around $150 million per year from 1984 through 1986. The excess of taxes over benefits during that period remained too low to restore the trust fund balance.

West Virginia considered issuing bonds during 1987 and issued $259 million in serial revenue bonds on September 1st. The issue completely repaid the state's outstanding Title XII loans. Subsequently, its trust fund was rebuilt somewhat. The balance reached $146 million at the end of 1989 and remained near $150 million through 1996.

At the time of the bond issue, West Virginia planned to repay the bonds over a six-year period. The bonds for the final two years, 1992 and 1993, were all callable. Financing came from two sources: a flat-rate employee payroll tax of 0.35 percent on the total UI-covered wages and an equivalent-yielding flat-rate employer payroll tax levied on the first $21,000 of annual earnings. Those taxes yielded sufficient revenues between 1988 and 1991 to complete West Virginia's repayments by July 1991, two years earlier than anticipated. The administrative costs of collecting the taxes were paid from the state's UI administrative allocation, which it received from the UI Service.

West Virginia's trust fund balance in recent years, roughly $150 million, is not large when compared to the state's past rates of benefit payouts. Note the 1982 and 1983 levels of benefit payments: $234 and $259 million, respectively. The level of the state's trust fund is not high enough to prevent renewed borrowing. The 1996 level of reserves was $157 million (see Table 1-4). The associated 1996 reserve ratio multiple was only 0.33, the fifth lowest in the United States and roughly half of the national average.

Table 4-3 Summary of West Virginia's UI Trust Fund Activities, 1979 to 1994[a] ($ millions)

	UI trust fund flows			UI trust fund reserves			Title XII loans			State bonds	
Year	Taxes	Interest	Benefits	Gross reserves	Net reserves	U.S. Treasury debt	Loans	Repayments	Debt	Scheduled repayments	Bond taxes
1979	81	3	101	39	39	0	0	0	0	NA[b]	NA
1980	79	0	158	3	−44	47	47	0	47	NA	NA
1981	131	0	150	29	−71	100	53	0	100	NA	NA
1982	166	0	234	0	−144	144	45	1	144	NA	NA
1983	142	0	259	0	−288	288	152	8	288	NA	NA
1984	150	0	146	33	−275	308	37	17	308	NA	NA
1985	149	0	145	0	−256	256	44	96	256	NA	NA
1986	150	0	143	0	−225	225	102	132	225	NA	NA
1987	152	1	114	65	65	0	40	265	0	0	0
1988	157	9	98	133	133	0	0	0	0	30	60
1989	100	12	91	146	146	0	0	0	0	37	62
1990	86	13	92	153	153	0	0	0	0	43	67
1991	104	12	146	157	157	0	0	0	0	46	68
1992	112	11	138	141	141	0	0	0	0	49	0
1993	119	11	117	155	155	0	0	0	0	53	0
1994	122	10	125	162	162	0	0	0	0	0	0

SOURCE: Data on trust fund transactions, including Title XII loans, is from the U.S. Department of Labor. Data on the scheduled repayment of state bonds is from the state of West Virginia. Estimates of state bond taxes are made by the author.
[a] Reserves and debt are measured at the year end.
[b] NA = not applicable, as state bonds were issued in 1987.

Connecticut entered the 1990s with a small UI trust fund balance of $274 million. Its reserve ratio multiple, 0.22 at the end of 1989, was the second lowest in the United States. The state's unemployment rate had dropped below 4.0 percent in every year between 1986 and 1989 but rose to 5.2, 6.8, 7.6, and 6.3 percent from 1990 through 1993. While its unemployment rates were not noticeably higher than the U.S. national average, increases in unemployment in the late 1980s were greater in Connecticut. Annual UI benefit payments from 1990 through 1993 averaged $519 million, compared with $196 million from 1986 through 1989.

The state's UI trust fund was exhausted at the end of 1990. Borrowing from the U.S. Treasury totaled $502 million in 1991, $502 million 1992, and $363 million in 1993. Total indebtedness was $760 million at the end of July 1993.

In mid 1993, Connecticut enacted solvency legislation that increased employer taxes, reduced benefits, and authorized the issuing of state revenue bonds to pay its outstanding debts to the U.S. Treasury. The legislation included substantial increases in the taxable wage base, an increase in the solvency tax associated with regular UI taxation, and a special tax assessment, starting in 1994, to pay off the state bonds.[26] Benefit reductions included a change in the computation of the weekly benefit amount, increased penalties for "willful misconduct" disqualifications, broadened severance pay disqualifications, and a lower monetary threshold for "larceny" disqualifications.

The legislation established a new Unemployment Compensation Advance Fund for revenues from the bond issues plus employer bond assessments (taxes) and investment income. The fund pays the administrative costs of bond issues and the costs of collecting bond taxes.

Connecticut issued a total of about $1.0 billion in revenue bonds between August and September 1993. The issues included both fixed-maturity and callable bonds. The proceeds of the bond issues completely repaid the outstanding debt to the U.S. Treasury.[27] Special bond tax assessments started in August 1994, and bond repayments began in November 1994. Scheduled repayments are to occur at six-month intervals through the year 2001. However, the callable bonds may be paid off earlier.

By the end of 1996, $154 million of the total issues had been repaid. This included $115 million in scheduled repayments and $39 million in repayments of callable bonds.[28] Fixed-maturity obligations will continue to fall due through 2001, so a full evaluation of the success of the bond issue cannot be made at this time.

Connecticut's bond issues were timed to avoid interest charges on borrowing from January to September 1993. The state considered several options, but then issued a series of bonds and notes rather than instruments of shorter duration, such as tax-free commercial paper. There were three types of bonds: fixed-rate, synthetic fixed-rate, and variable-rate, with the latter accounting for about one-third of the total.[29] Repayment of the fixed-rate bonds began in November 1994 and is scheduled to last through November 2001. Callable issues falling due between 1998 and 2001 can be called earlier than their maturity dates.

The interest rates on Connecticut's bonds and notes range from 2.75 percent to about 5.0 percent. As shown in Table 4-1, the 1993 interest rate on Title XII borrowing was 7.45 percent. Clearly, Connecticut saved on the interest rate it actually paid. To this point, it appears that the bond issues were over-financed, and revenues in excess of the amounts needed to repay its fixed-bond obligations then became available to repay its callable bonds.[30] However, it is not obvious that Connecticut will realize a net saving on its total interest charges. The question of savings on total interest charges can be more fully addressed when all of Connecticut's debt has been repaid.

Despite the bond issues, Connecticut has modestly rebuilt its UI trust fund. The fund balance at the end of 1996 was $278 million (see Table 1-4), and the reserve ratio multiple was only 0.18, or slightly lower than it had been at the end of 1989, just before the downturn of the 1990s. At the end of 1996, Connecticut had a substantial outstanding state-issued debt and only a modest UI trust fund balance. The fiscal condition of the state's UI program was not strong.[31]

Three conclusions emerge from the experiences of Louisiana, West Virginia, and Connecticut:

- All had low levels of UI trust fund reserves when the recessions began. When high unemployment caused large drawdowns of their trust funds, all quickly developed large debts and then resorted to an innovative form of financing—bond issues.

- Louisiana and West Virginia repaid their debts more rapidly than either had anticipated at the time of the bond issues. This was also true for Connecticut, at least through mid 1997. The bond programs can be described as "over-financed," in as much as the anticipated annual tax revenues exceeded the annual retirement of the fixed-maturity debt contemplated at the time the bonds were issued.

- After issuing bonds to pay off UI indebtedness, the three states had different experiences with UI trust fund accumulation. Connecticut and West Virginia have not rebuilt their UI trust fund balances to high levels. Both states may need Title XII loans during the next recession. From 1993 through 1996, Louisiana raised its UI trust fund balance substantially. The state's reserve ratio multiple stood at 1.10 at the end of 1996, or 72 percent above the national average. It appears that both Connecticut and West Virginia need to improve the basic balance between UI program revenues and benefit payments. Innovative borrowing arrangements are no substitute for underlying financial soundness in UI program financing.

THE ADVANTAGES AND DISADVANTAGES
OF THE ALTERNATIVES

To help compare different methods of debt financing, this section reviews four topics. Three deal directly with the costs of indebtedness, and the fourth also has cost implications. The discussion repeats some points made earlier but emphasizes a comparison of the alternatives.

Interest Rate Spreads

Many types of state debt can be issued. This discussion is confined to the interest rates on the four types of debt discussed earlier (see Table 4-1) and the associated interest-rate spreads. The four are Title XII loans, Aaa municipal bonds, six-month taxable commercial paper, and one-month tax-free commercial paper. The latter two are proxies for short-term interest rates, but it should be noted that the gamut of short-term instruments runs from one-month commercial paper to three-year notes.

As noted earlier, Title XII rates have consistently exceeded Aaa municipal bond rates since 1983, with the spread being variable but often larger when interest rates are lower. The spread between Aaa municipal bonds and six-month taxable commercial paper also varies widely, but it is generally smaller than the Title XII-Aaa spread. Between 1989 and 1996, however, the spread ranged from −181 basis points (1989) to 229 basis points (1992). Even larger spreads occur between Aaa municipal bond rates and the rates on one-month tax-free commercial paper. In 1992, the spread was 347 basis, but it exceeded 200 basis points in each of the six years from 1991 through 1996 and in nine of the last eleven years (see Table 4-1). Even greater volatility in interest rate spreads would appear if monthly data were examined.

For the foreseeable future, Title XII rates are likely to exceed Aaa municipal bond rates. It also is highly likely that interest rates on very short-term instruments will remain far below Aaa municipal bond rates. Moreover, as shown in Table 4-1, annual interest rate spreads vary widely. The differences are even greater and more varied in the monthly data. If cost comparisons could be made solely on the basis of interest rates, Title XII rates would clearly be the highest and short-term tax-free rates the lowest.

The Costs of Issues

The costs of issuing affect the relative attractiveness of state debt. There are no underwriting fees on Title XII loans from the U.S. Treasury. Underwriting fees vary according to the type of state debt instrument and are generally higher for longer-term obligations, higher for obligations with call features, higher for smaller issues, and higher for revenue bonds than they are for general obligation bonds.[32]

An appropriate comparison of state debt and Title XII loans would add issuing fees to the interest rate for each type of instrument. The fees make state debt more expensive and raise the interest rate spread required to save on the costs of state debt issues.

The Costs of Debt Repayment

At present, states can treat the administrative costs of debt repayment identically under each of the four alternatives. Title XII loans repaid by state payroll taxes have their administrative costs defrayed by the administrative finance allocation from the U.S. Department of Labor. According to current interpretations, administrative finance allocations can also be used to defray the cost of collecting the state bond taxes levied to repay state-issued debt instruments. There may be small differences in the scale of the state-tax-related costs, but states can treat this aspect of tax administration like any other UI tax collection.

Of the three states that have issued state debt instruments, only one, West Virginia, has used its UI administrative allocation to cover the cost of collecting bond taxes. Connecticut's reliance on its own resources is especially interesting, given that it received a written interpretation that federal monies could be used to collect bond taxes.

Note, too, that the federal monies distributed to states for UI program administration can be used to pay for the administration of a purely state tax. This suggests a question: if states can issue tax-exempt bonds to minimize their interest costs, why should the federal government pay for the costs of administering such state taxes? If the current federal interpretation were to change, the cost of issuing state debt would also have to include administrative costs.

Positions on the question vary, and at the end of 1996, that of the UI Service differed from that of Louisiana officials in 1987. As noted, Louisiana law explicitly provided for state financing to administer its state tax, through an annual transfer from the trust account to the state's Department of Labor. West Virginia had no such provision. Connecticut, despite having received written authorization to use its federal UI administrative allocation to collect bond taxes, opted to use its own resources.

Flexibility

Flexibility in borrowing and repaying clearly differs according to the method of debt financing. Title XII loans and repayments can and do take place daily. Essentially, the process operates on demand for debtor states, allowing them to maintain a zero balance, which minimizes the average amount of outstanding debt.

· State debt issues, however, are inherently less flexible than Title XII borrowing. States must plan for an issue and must have contingency plans, for unexpected developments can alter the projected time paths for benefit payments, tax receipts, and/or interest rates. Unexpected developments affecting receipts and expenditures (hence affecting the trust fund balance) can be addressed in two ways: by issuing short-term debt and by issuing callable long-term debt. Most forms of issuing debt require preparation time, but it is possible to issue commercial paper daily.

Another aspect of flexibility is the ability to call bonds. After bonds have been issued to pay off Title XII loans, any excess in a state's annual bond tax receipts over its maturing fixed-maturity bonds can be used to repay callable bonds.

Including callable bonds in a state debt issue gives the state the ability to speed up its debt repayment if its economy performs better than anticipated. Issuing callable bonds also provides flexibility when performance falls below anticipation. Uncertainty can be addressed by making the total issue larger than the state's "best" estimate of its borrowing needs. However, this strategy has its costs, i.e., the interest charges and costs of issuing for any "excess" bonds.

Alternatively, the state can resort to new debt issues as needed. Following this strategy would mean the first issue would be smaller, but the cost of a potential second issue would also have to be considered.

Thus, while Title XII loans are clearly the most flexible, issuing short-term state debt, issuing of callable bonds, and planning for a second debt issue also offer considerable flexibility.

UNCERTAINTIES FOR DEBTOR STATES

A state faces several uncertainties when it considers how best to finance its UI debt. This section reviews some of the uncertainties already noted and adds other considerations.

The future performance of the state's economy is an obvious uncertainty affecting the volume and timing of borrowing. Unexpected increases in unemployment raise benefit outlays and reduce tax receipts. There are also uncertainties about interest rate spreads.

What has not been emphasized up to this point, however, is the uncertainty associated with state and federal legislation. A state facing debt or additional debt may enact legislation designed to improve solvency. In such situations, the volume of future indebtedness will be reduced or eliminated. The three states that have used bond issues enacted solvency legislation at the time the bond issue was authorized. All three states were already substantially indebted to the U.S. Treasury.

Developments in Maine, a state facing first-time borrowing during early 1993, are instructive. Actuarial projections made at the end of 1992 showed borrowing would begin in early 1993 and would be chronic for the rest of the 1990s.[33] After some deliberation, Maine crafted temporary legislation that included an emergency solvency tax, an increase in the maximum tax rate, a continuation of a freeze on the maximum benefit, and a reduction in weekly benefits for new claimants. The legislation, effective during 1993 and 1994, was designed to avoid major indebtedness for that period, build a modest balance by the end of 1994, and give Maine time to develop a long-term solution to its UI funding imbalance. The temporary legislation became effective on April 1st, but its tax provisions were retroactive to January 1st. A two-year improvement in solvency was expected. The improvement totaled $60 million, with tax increases accounting for about 80 percent. Because of the legislation, Maine did not accumulate a large debt during 1993 and 1994. Subsequently, Maine enacted other solvency measures in 1995, 1996, and 1997.

Experiences in Massachusetts in the early 1990s also illustrate how legislation can affect the scale of future debt. Provisions of 1991 legislation that came into effect in 1992 included a higher taxable wage base, a higher maximum tax rate schedule, and selected benefit reductions. As a result, tax receipts grew substantially in 1992. Whatever the previous prospect had been, Massachusetts anticipated that its debt accumulation would be smaller following the 1991 legislation. The bond issuance that had been considered before to the 1991 legislation did not take place. The state's indebtedness to the U.S. Treasury fell during 1993, and all loans were fully repaid in May 1994.

Federal legislation can also affect a state's decisions about whether to issue debt instruments. The uncertainties are of a different magnitude, however. State preferences are not as influential in framing UI legislation and/or administrative guidelines at the federal level. One can argue that current federal guidelines favor state debt issues over Title XII borrowing. There are three factors to look at here, each of which could change.[34]

First, states can "game" the Title XII cash-flow borrowing procedures. Cash-flow loans were originally intended to cover low trust fund balances, where tax receipts and benefit outlays are roughly equal but differ in their seasonal patterns. Thus, borrowing and repayment would roughly balance over the fiscal year, leaving no debt on September 30th. Foregoing federal interest charges associated with cash-flow borrowing can be justified. However, at present, a state may borrow repeatedly during the fiscal year, accumulate a sizeable debt, and then issue a state debt instrument to pay off all borrowing on September 30th. The state avoids all federal interest charges on the debt accumulated through September 30th and starts to pay interest on the state debt issued on September 30th. This use of cash-flow borrowing differs from the intended use.

Second, a state can use its federal grant for UI program administration to defray the cost of collecting the state taxes used to retire state-issued debt. If the debt is truly state debt and hence is eligible for tax-free status, why should a state be allowed to use federal monies to administer the collection of a state tax?[35] As noted, Louisiana and Connecticut used state resources to defray these costs of tax administration, but West Virginia used its federal UI administrative allocation.

Third, the current interpretation of the trust fund withdrawal standard on repaying state-issued debt can be questioned. At present, if a state issues debt and then deposits the proceeds into its trust fund account, it may later make withdrawals from the trust fund to repay the principal on the loan.[36] The argument behind this interpretation is that since the principal was used to pay benefits, repaying the principal is a use of the trust fund for the same purpose.

In the three areas outlined, the current federal administrative guidelines confer financial and/or administrative advantages on states that issue state debt instead of using Title XII loans. Given the federal budget deficit and the pressure to reduce it, it is conceivable that the UI Service, the Secretary of Labor, or the Office of Management and Budget could change one or more of the guidelines. If there were changes, the relative cost of issuing state debt would be higher in the future.

To summarize, though uncertainties about the economy and about interest rate spreads are clearly important, the potential for changes in both the state and federal legislation must also be taken in to account. Further, current federal administrative interpretations could change. Any of these uncertainties can affect a state's decision about the best way to repay its trust fund indebtedness.

SOME COST COMPARISONS

The main reason for issuing state debt is to save on interest costs. This section compares the cost of state bond issues and Title XII loans for Louisiana and West Virginia, the two states that have repaid their state-issued bonds. The summary information presented is based on annual spreadsheet models for the bond issues and for Title XII loans.

To keep the discussion focused, the comparisons involve states that have long-term debts rather than states that are just starting to incur debts. The comparisons are illustrative but do not attempt to convey the full reality. The emphasis is on three factors: interest rate differentials, the duration of indebtedness, and the share of the bond issue deposited in the state's UI trust fund.

Each of the three factors deserves some elaboration. The interest rates on a bond issue are fixed over the course of the debt, but Title XII interest rates vary by year. The comparisons made here use a single interest rate for both, the average rate applicable on the first year of bond repayments. Because the Title XII interest rate can rise or fall from its first-year level, a comparison based on constant rates might violate reality, but it does not necessarily bias the results.

Two factors determine the duration of indebtedness: the size of the state's initial debt and the annual excess of its revenues (regular UI taxes plus the state taxes used to repay the bonds, hereafter known as "bond taxes") over UI benefit payments during the repayment period.

The simulations for both methods of financing use past levels of UI trust fund tax receipts plus estimates for bond taxes.[37]

Any state issuing bonds must use some part of the proceeds to cover interest charges, issuing fees, administration, and contingencies. Unlike Title XII borrowing, a part of the loan proceeds is not deposited directly into the UI trust fund. Louisiana and West Virginia provided information on those amounts.

The simulation follows certain assumptions for both states. Under Title XII, the excess of tax revenues over UI benefits went first to repay outstanding loans and then to build the trust fund. Thus, the debt was paid off faster under Title XII, but because the trust fund balance was zero in the early years, the fund did not start to earn interest income as quickly. Both Title XII borrowing and state debt issuing eventually resulted in positive trust fund balances and trust fund interest earnings.

Table 4-4 provides summary information for Louisiana and West Virginia under the two alternatives. Louisiana borrowed $1,315 million and deposited only about $820 million directly into its UI trust fund,[38] with the remainder going to related trust accounts. The deposit ratio (0.624) is low, but at the time there was great uncertainty about the state's need for additional loans.

As noted, the state's bonds were fully defrayed during 1993, and bond repayments were completed during 1994. The simulation indicates that Louisiana's bond taxes generated a total of $1,357 million between 1987 and 1993.[39] Thus, the simulation agrees with reality in that the last of the debt was covered six years after the issue. Given equivalent tax revenues during those years (including bond taxes), however, the debt would have been fully repaid in 1990 under Title XII, and the trust fund balance would have reached $740.8 rather than $601.0 million by the end of 1992.

Note the interest totals for the two methods of financing. Bond issues earned Louisiana's trust fund $150.1 million, but total interest costs on the bonds were $224.3 million and net interest costs were $74.2 million. Under Title XII, the comparable totals were $116.5 million in Title XII interest charges, $89.9 million in trust fund interest earnings, and a net cost of $26.6 million, or $47.6 million less than for the bond issue.[40]

In the simulations, Louisiana had larger net interest charges and a smaller trust fund end balance when it issued bonds. This result

Table 4-4 Comparisons of Bond Issues and Title XII Loans for Louisiana and West Virginia[a]

| | Louisiana | | West Virginia | |
	State bonds	Title XII	State bonds	Title XII
Total bond issues	1,315	NA[b]	258	NA
Bonds deposited in UI trust fund	820	NA	226	NA
Deposits/total issues	0.624	NA	0.876	NA
Issuance year	1987	NA	1987	NA
Year of full debt repayment	1993	1990	1991	1989
Interest rate	0.0680	0.0933	0.0680	0.0933
Interest on borrowing	224.3	116.5	32.5	22.8
Trust fund interest	150.1	89.9	58.5	22.1
Net interest paid	74.2	26.6	−26.0	0.7
Trust fund balance, December 31, 1992	601.0	740.8	141.0	119.6

SOURCE: Based on simulations by the author.
[a] All dollar amounts are measured in millions.
[b] NA = not applicable, as the state already had Title XII debts and all borrowing had been deposited in the state's UI trust fund.

obtained even though the bond interest rate was 253 basis points lower than the Title XII interest rate. The explanation lies in the combination the low deposit-to-total-issuance ratio (0.624) and the longer average time over which interest charges accrued on the bonds. Bond interest was paid for six years (1988 through 1993), but Title XII interest was paid only through 1990.

Different results were obtained for West Virginia even though the simulations used the same interest rates as for Louisiana. The deposit-to-total-issuance ratio was higher (0.876) and West Virginia's bonds were paid off much more rapidly (in four years rather than six). The interest paid on the debt was somewhat larger under bond issue ($32.5 million versus $22.8 million), but larger trust fund interest earnings also accrued ($58.5 million versus $22.1 million). West Virginia paid net interest of $0.7 million under Title XII borrowing, compared to net interest earnings of $26.0 million under bond issuance. Also note that the December 1992 fund balance was higher under the bond issue ($141.0 million versus $119.6 million).[41]

Are interest costs lower under bond issues? It depends. For West Virginia, the bond issue meant savings on interest costs and a higher trust fund balance at the end of 1992. For Louisiana, the results were the opposite. The two principal reasons for the contrast are that Louisiana deposited a smaller share of its total bond issue in its UI trust fund and that it had a longer period of indebtedness.

It must be emphasized that the simulations assumed away certain complications. The interest rate spreads are held to be constant. When the states decided to issue bonds, in 1987, both states had long-term trust fund indebtedness. Thus, the simulations do not take into account cash-flow borrowing (and the associated interest-forgiveness under Title XII) or decisions about the length of the debt instruments to issue. The simulations also assume identical revenue streams for Title XII loans and state bond issues within each state.

SUMMARY

The question of how to finance UI trust fund debts is complex, and the appropriate route for a state depends on several factors. Two states, Louisiana and West Virginia, issued bonds in the 1987 to pay off accumulated trust fund debts and used state payroll taxes to repay the bonds. A third state, Connecticut, opted for a bond issue in 1993. However, the experiences of these three states represent but a small fraction of the possibilities for issuing state debt as an alternative to Title XII loans.

There are eight factors that a state must consider in reaching a prudent decision about the best way to finance its UI trust fund debt:

1. Anticipated future state economic performance

2. The possibility of state solvency legislation

3. Federal legislation and administrative guidelines on state debt issues

4. The expected duration of indebtedness

5. The flexibility of daily borrowing and repayment under Title XII

6. The availability of Title XII cash-flow loans

7. Interest rate spreads across various debt instruments, and

8. Underwriting fees and other costs of issuing state debt.

Four of these factors merit additional comment.

- Factor 1: Both the anticipated rate of growth and the degree of uncertainty about future growth affect debt financing. If strong economic growth is anticipated, then the there is less need to issue long-term bonds, for the state can anticipate a rapid recovery of its trust fund balance through future revenues associated with economic growth. Large debts coupled with uncertainty about future growth, on the other hand, increase the appeal of state bond issues.

- Factor 2: If solvency legislation looks likely, the need to address debt financing with long-term bond issues is less pressing; the solvency legislation itself would provide most of remedy for the state's debt problem. However, the political situation many make a sharp increase in experience-rated employer taxes unattractive, thus increasing the likelihood of long-term indebtedness. Bond issues might then have more appeal. Note that this factor overlaps with the expected duration of indebtedness. Solvency provisions were included in the three state laws that provided for bond issues. Solvency legislation was also a primary factor in obviating the need for bond issues in Maine and Massachusetts.

- Factor 7: The point here is that the range of potential debt instruments extends far beyond a simple comparison of, for example, the Aaa municipal bond rate and the Title XII interest rate. The term structure of interest rates, the tax treatment of bond interest income, and the issuing costs for different debt instruments are all important.

- Factor 8: To the extent there are economies of scale in issuing state debt, larger states and states with higher ratios of debt to covered wages (more serious debt problems) would find debt issues more attractive than would smaller states and states with a smaller scale of indebtedness.

During the next recession, some states will undoubtedly seriously consider issuing the state UI debt.

Notes

1. This chapter is based on a report to the U.S. Department of Labor (Vroman 1993).
2. Details of the patterns of UI debt repayment in the 1970s and 1980s are given in Vroman (1990), Chapter 1.
3. There are some exceptions to this statement—for example, tax refunds for overpayments and small amounts originally deposited in state trust funds during the 1950s, under the Reed Act—but they are minor.
4. The Secretary of Labor must be satisfied that the funds used to pay interest on a state's trust fund debts do not come, directly or indirectly, from the state's trust fund account. In making this determination, the Secretary requires debtor states to identify the source of funds for interest payments and the statutory basis for the establishment and use of funds for making interest payments. See U.S. Department of Labor (1988).
5. The fourth-quarter interest rate is the interest rate paid on investments in special certificates of indebtedness issued by the U.S. Treasury to the Unemployment Trust Fund. The interest rate for these special debt instruments is the average rate for outstanding Treasury interest-bearing obligations with maturities of four years or more.
6. This interest payment is due the day after the first day of borrowing during the October–December period. The interest on borrowing between October 1st and December 31st is due at the end of the next fiscal year, September 30th.
7. States typically require payments by the end of the month following the end of a calendar quarter, a 30- or 31-day delay. Employers usually make tax payments on the last day possible, and there are usually a few days before the trust fund accounts register the deposits.
8. See Vroman (1993), Table 1 and the associated text, for added details on the two states.

9. The Massachusetts economy is about twice the size of the Connecticut economy. Taxable covered employment in 1988, for example, was 2.53 million in Massachusetts, compared with 1.37 million in Connecticut. If the funding imbalances were proportionate to each state's economy, Massachusetts would be expected to borrow about twice as much as Connecticut.

10. Debt repayments (including complete repayment) between November 10th and the end of the year do not prevent the penalty. There is no avoidance feature analogous to the interest avoidance feature of cash-flow borrowing repaid by September 30th.

11. The technical phrase for the penalty tax rate is the "FUTA tax credit offset rate." States with acceptable experience-rating systems may impose experience-rated taxes on their employers in lieu of a flat 5.4 percent state tax. In the first year of automatic debt repayment, the maximum permissible tax credit offset rate is 5.1 percent, hence a 0.3 percent additional federal tax rate.

12. Annual increases in the FUTA penalty tax rate after the first year of penalty taxes depend on state-specific circumstances. The increase in the second year may be an additional 0.3 percent (for a total federal tax rate of 1.4 percent) or larger.

13. An advisory directive from the U.S. Department of Labor indicates that the states can use their financial allocation for UI program administration to collect both the separate and the regular UI payroll taxes. The added administrative expenses do not have to be financed separately.

14. There are 100 basis points per full percentage point in an interest rate.

15. Interest was first charged on U.S. Treasury loans after April 1, 1982. The Title XII rates before 1982 have been calculated in the same way as the rates charged on interest-bearing loans. The interest rate (specified in paragraph 904(b) of the Social Security Act) is the average rate on public debt for the last three months of the preceding calendar year.

16. See Miller, Pavosevich, and Vroman (1997) and Vroman (1990) for summaries of borrowing and repayment patterns.

17. Of course, Title XII and other federal statutes governing UI-related borrowing and repayment must be satisfied. Administrative rulings by the U.S. Treasury make it difficult for states to issue bonds in anticipation of future indebtedness.

18. General obligation bonds are backed by the full financial resources of the issuer. Revenue bonds are backed by a specific asset or tax base. In borrowing to pay off UI trust fund debts, a state would be expected to issue revenue bonds or other debt secured by future payroll taxes on UI covered employment. Callable bonds have a stated maturity date but, under stated conditions, allow the issuer to redeem them earlier. A call could occur either because the excess of revenues over benefits surpassed expectations or because changes in interest rates favor the issue of another type of debt instrument. The owner of callable bonds usually receives a higher interest rate for those bonds relative to fixed bonds of the same maturity. Notes often have maturities of six months to three years, while commercial paper typically covers one to six months.

19. To compare the issuing fees for different classes of debt instruments and of instruments of differing maturities, a state would need to make assumptions about several features of each instrument being considered. The issuing fees for bonds, notes, and commercial paper shown in the text should be seen as illustrating likely ranges.

20. The legislation in Maine that became effective April 1, 1993, is a good example of state action motivated by a desire to avoid insolvency. A two-year emergency package raised taxes retroactive to January 1, 1993, and reduced benefits, starting in April 1993. This legislation is discussed below.

21. See Miller, Pavosevich, and Vroman (1997), Table 9.3.

22. From 1980 through 1983, the national unemployment rate averaged 8.5 percent of the labor force. The corresponding four-year averages for Louisiana and West Virginia were 9.3 and 13.0 percent, respectively. During the next four years, 1984 through 1987, the national unemployment rate averaged 7.0 percent, but Louisiana's averaged 11.7 percent, and West Virginia's averaged 12.7 percent.

23. The disparities between benefits and taxes for 1982 and 1983 are even larger than suggested in Table 4-2. The benefit data do not include the state's share of extended benefit payments, which totaled $15 million and $53 million, respectively.

24. The tax was first collected in the last half of 1987. For that year, the taxable wage base was $7,500.

25. Of the monies deposited into the benefit transfer account, only about $40 million was used to defray additional borrowing from the U.S. Treasury. The bulk of the account was eventually used to retire bonds.

26. The taxable wage base rose from $7,100 in 1993 to $9,000 in 1994 and was slated to rise by annual increments of $1,000, reaching $13,000 in 1998, and then to rise to $15,000 in 1999. The solvency tax rate rose from 1.0 percent in 1993 to 1.5 percent from 1994 through 1998, and then was scheduled to drop to 1.4 percent in 1999. The taxes to repay the bonds were to be levied as a portion of each employer's experience rate and were estimated to average from 0.75 percent to 1.05 percent on the taxable wages paid in the experience-year ending the June 30th prior to the tax year.

27. The bond proceeds were also used to pay benefits from late September 1993 through early April 1994, at which time first-quarter regular contributions became available.

28. Repayments through July 1997 totaled $224 million, with $155 million in scheduled repayments and $69 million in callable bonds.

29. Synthetic fixed-rate bonds can be described as fixed for the state but variable for the underwriter. In other words, the underwriter undertook the risk of varying the interest rates to be paid to bondholders. These bonds were refunded during 1996 and replaced with a true fixed-rate issue.

30. This was anticipated in planning Connecticut's bond issues. Borrowing less would have meant risking failing to meet the repayment schedule for the fixed-maturity debt.

31. A factor that will inhibit future trust fund building is a tax provision that reduces the solvency tax when the trust fund balance (the net of all borrowing) exceeds 0.8 percent of total wages. This threshold was $377 million at the end of 1996.

32. Issues that are not insured (or secured by some other means) have lower underwriting fees, but such savings are largely or totally offset by the higher interest associated with a greater risk of default.

33. Like many states, Maine has an indexed weekly benefit maximum but a fixed taxable wage base. During the 1990–1992 recession, which was especially severe throughout New England, the state's trust fund balance was almost exhausted. In fact, Table 1-4 shows that the 1989–1992 decline in Maine's reserve ratio multiple was the largest for all 53 UI programs.

34. The discussion that follows represents the opinions of the author. To the author's knowledge, the U.S. Department of Labor has no plans to revise its administrative guidelines for state debt issues. Some readers may consider the guidelines entirely appropriate, but others may argue that the guidelines are not neutral in their effect on decisions about state debt issues.

35. There are many points of view on this issue. One perspective (more sympathetic to UI programs issuing state debt) can be expressed as follows. If issuing state debt is an option, then the administrative costs of collecting the associated taxes should be reimbursable, since the ultimate purpose of such taxes is to finance the payment of UI benefits.

36. This interpretation was articulated in a letter dated March 29, 1993, from the UI Service to the Director of Accounts of the Connecticut Department of Labor.

37. In effect, the assumption is that under the Title XII alternative the state levies additional flat-rate payroll taxes. These taxes have an annual yield equal to the bond tax receipts and remain in effect for the same number of years.

38. The $820 million consisted of $780 million deposited at the time of the bond issue and another $40 million deposited to cover additional borrowing during the following months.

39. The $1,357 million represents about 70 percent of the state's regular UI taxes for the seven years. Note the tax receipts for 1987 to 1993 in Table 4-2.

40. For both Louisiana and West Virginia, the interest costs for bond issues cover all years that bonds were outstanding (through 1993 in Louisiana). The UI trust fund interest earnings totals cover the years through 1992.

41. The summary for West Virginia is carried through 1992, even though it completed its state bonds repayment in 1991. This was done partly to compare the results with those for Louisiana. The general findings on bond issues versus Title XII borrowing do not change for West Virginia when the analysis stops at the end of 1991. Under the bond issue, the 1991 trust fund end balance is higher ($157 million versus $137 million) and the net interest cost is lower (net interest earnings of $14.5 million versus net interest payments of $10.8 million).

5 State Reserve Funds

State reserve funds are a recent UI policy initiative.[1] Reserve funds are created by the partial redirection of employer UI taxes into specially administered state accounts. The principal in these state accounts is dedicated to the payment of UI benefits. However, the interest income from reserve funds can be used in several ways: to help unemployed workers find new jobs and to help finance UI and/or employment service (ES) administrative activities.

A state's financing situation can make the creation of a reserve fund attractive and feasible.

1. Total reserves in the UI trust fund accounts at the U.S. Treasury are high in many states, not only in absolute levels but also relative to the size of the state economies. Several states judge these balances to be fully adequate for financing drawdowns in a future recession.

2. Under the UI trust fund withdrawal standard, monies held in the U.S. Treasury accounts can be used only to pay UI benefits. This standard applies to interest earnings on trust fund balances, to the principal, and to new deposits.

3. States are increasingly recognizing that training and other adjustment activities can speed the reemployment of unemployed workers. By easing the transition to new jobs, such state-supported initiatives may also help UI trust funds to realize savings through reduced benefit outlays.

4. State Employment Security Agencies (SESAs) are finding it increasingly difficult to cover their traditional UI and ES administrative functions with only the federal allocations made available for those purposes. Many states now supplement their federal SESA administrative allocations with monies from other sources. In some states, this supplement takes the form of a supplemental payroll tax on UI-covered employers.

Taken together, these situations make the establishment of a state reserve fund attractive. By creating a reserve fund, the state can, in effect, gain access to interest earnings that would otherwise lie in its U.S. Treasury account, earnings dedicated solely to paying future benefits.

This chapter addresses several questions about creating a state reserve fund and how such a fund functions, including its relation to the UI trust fund account at the U.S. Treasury and its effect on the solvency of a state's UI program. The chapter does not offer definitive answers to these questions. It does provide partial answers and also provides information important for answering other questions.

The chapter's three main conclusions are

- State reserve funds represent an alternative use for interest earnings that would otherwise go only to paying benefits.

- A state that creates a reserve fund and maintains its balance as intended in subsequent years does not significantly increase its risk of UI program insolvency. (This conclusion is based partly on simulations using a model of Indiana's UI program, which evaluated a 1991 proposal to establish a reserve fund.)

- Regulatory oversight does not, at present, ensure that state reserve funds remain dedicated to paying benefits.

A DESCRIPTION OF STATE RESERVE FUNDS

State reserve funds are created by partially redirecting employer taxes from their usual destination (the state UI trust fund account at the U.S. Treasury) to a special fund set up and administered by the state. The reserve fund accumulates assets for several years, until it reaches the target level specified in the authorizing legislation. The principal in the reserve fund remains dedicated to the payment of UI benefits, not by directly issuing checks to claimants, but by acting as a reinsurance fund that can make advances to the state's account at the U.S. Treasury should that account become depleted. In contrast to the current situation, where UI programs borrow from the Federal Unemployment Account (the FUA), a state with a reserve fund borrows first from itself and then from the FUA. Borrowing from the FUA occurs only if the reserve fund is fully loaned out or has already reached an unacceptably low level.

The reserve fund's principal is invested in secure assets, for example, U.S. Treasury bonds that generate interest income. States administer these investment decisions and thus control the level of risk in reserve fund financial assets. The interest income can be used in two general ways: for promoting worker adjustments in the labor market and for administering either the UI or the ES program, or both. Since a new state tax is created, some monies must also be dedicated to collecting reserve fund taxes. The authorizing legislation therefore specifies that some part of reserve fund interest income be used to defray the cost of administering the reserve fund.

The uses of reserve fund interest for worker adjustments and for administering UI and/or ES can vary. The potential range of training, for example, is suggested by the following target groups: workers recently unemployed or at substantial risk of unemployment; dislocated workers; UI benefit exhaustees and other long-term unemployed; persons who do not qualify for other federal or state job training programs; employers seeking to recruit workers in new and expanding industries and occupations; employers facing critical skill shortages in selected occupations; employers considering a plant closing unless the costs of worker retraining can be at least partially covered by a public program; and worker upgrading. Potential trainees would vary in terms of their employability and their previous UI history. To the extent that a state training program hastens the reemployment of its UI claimants, the state may find itself with reduced UI benefit outlays.[2]

Reserve fund interest income is also directed to administering UI or ES programs, or both. Traditionally, both programs have been administered with federal monies allocated to the states under the Social Security Act and the Wagner-Peyser Act, respectively. Cutbacks in federal allocations mean that states must either reduce SESA employment and associated services or supplement federal grants with state monies. During 1996, at least five states levied a state payroll tax to increase monies available for UI and/or ES administration. Interest earnings from a state reserve fund can be another source of supplemental monies for administration.

LEGISLATIVE CONSIDERATIONS

The legislation that establishes a state reserve fund can vary in several respects, depending on the goals of the state. A state reserve fund can be set up to be tax- and revenue-neutral, or it can act as a flexible tax that automatically generates less revenue when reserves are high and more when reserves fall below a designated threshold.

For states that use the reserve ratio method of experience-rating to assign tax rates, a state reserve fund can have a significant effect on the total reserves. If a state has a reserve fund, the reserve calculation based on the federal fund balance would yield lower ratios and higher tax rates because part of the federal trust fund balance has been diverted to the reserve fund. A state that creates a reserve fund and continues to base its reserve ratio on the federal trust fund has an automatic tax rate increase. However, a reserve ratio based on total (federal plus state) reserves does not change, because part of the revenue is diverted to the state's reserve fund but total revenue within the system remains the same.[3]

During Indiana's 1991 deliberations on establishing a reserve fund, staff at the U.S. Department of Labor informed the state that legislation defining a tax rate based on total reserves might not conform to federal regulations. In other words, taxes designated for the federal trust fund should not be based on reserves outside the federal UI program. However, Indiana amended its proposed legislation and based its reserve ratio on federal UI tax revenue multiplied by 1.25, which effectively yielded a tax rate based on total reserves. This method for setting tax rates for experience-rated employers was approved by the Department of Labor. A state can also adjust the tax rate associated with each level of the federal reserve ratio, but such an adjustment is never exactly revenue-neutral. Even if it is known that federal trust fund revenue will decrease by a constant percentage each year (assuming that the federal tax reduction remains in force in years when the state reserve fund tax is inactive), future reserves will not decrease by a constant percentage.

For states that use benefit ratios, benefit-wage ratios, or declines in payrolls to experience-rate UI taxes, the balance in the state's reserve fund does not affect the experience-ratings for individual employers. However, many states using such experience-rating systems do use multiple tax rate schedules. In determining which schedule applies in a given year, the reserve level should refer only to the balance in the state's federal trust fund account.

As noted, it can be assumed that drawdowns on reserve fund balances would happen rarely, if at all. One way to define the maximum value or ceiling for a state's reserve fund is to peg it as a percentage of wages and salaries. The state's reserve fund tax would become inactive when state reserves reached that ceiling. Once the state reserve tax is inactive, the tax revenues can be eliminated or be redirected to the federal fund account. If revenues are redirected to the federal fund, the program remains revenue-neutral because the total tax rate remains unchanged: employers no longer have to pay the state tax rate, and they no longer receive the federal tax reduction.

If, on the other hand, the revenue is completely eliminated, the ceiling implies a tax reduction for employers in the years after the ceiling has been reached. Employers no longer pay the state reserve fund tax, and they continue to pay at an unchanging rate into the state trust fund at the U.S. Treasury. Lowering the ceiling level reduces total revenue and reserves and also generates earlier and more frequent tax cuts. If inactive state taxes are redirected, lowering the ceiling does not affect total reserves; it merely shifts the allocation between state and federal trust fund balances.

The flexible tax reduction described above is similar to other flexible tax features used by several states (discussed in Chapter 2). It generates additional revenue when a state's reserves (those not on loan) fall below a specified threshold. A state's reserve fund tax would be even more flexible if the ceiling on real reserves were flexible, e.g., if it were based on a minimum balance in the state's federal account and on a specified percentage of covered wages and salaries. A fund defined in this way would accumulate higher reserves during a downturn.[4] If the state's reserve fund tax were levied as a fraction of experience-rated taxes rather than at a flat rate, the fund would also accumulate reserves at a faster rate as the state's balance at the U.S. Treasury declined to lower levels. Employer experience-rated taxes would rise following an increase in unemployment and the associated increase in UI benefit payments. The increase in UI tax rates implies a higher tax rate for a state's reserve fund contributions. However, the reserve fund would not be subject to increases in benefit payouts and would accumulate higher reserves. Interest income generated by the fund would then increase, as higher unemployment led to higher tax rates and thus to larger deposits to the reserve fund.

There are few solvency implications for a reserve fund that specifically dedicates its principal to UI benefits. Total reserves and taxes (state plus federal) would remain nearly unchanged and would go to largely the same purpose, with the majority of future revenue deposited in the state's account at the U.S. Treasury and a percentage deposited in the state's reserve fund. The decrease in interest income earned by the federal trust fund account would depend on the percentage of future revenue diverted to the state's fund.[5] The state would, in turn, gain the use of interest income generated by its reserve fund.

States are free to choose the percentage of future revenues to be diverted to the reserve fund and to set the ceiling for the fund. The percentage diverted determines the rate at which the reserve fund grows. For a given percentage, the ceiling then determines the number of years that the reserve fund tax would be active. If the intention is to leave the level of total (federal plus state) reserves unchanged, the desired level of reserves in the fund would be influenced by the level of interest income targeted by the state.

However, if state tax revenue were not redirected to the federal account after the ceiling had been reached, the ceiling would determine the frequency of reductions in total taxes (more frequently with a lower ceiling), and the percentage diverted would determine the size of the reductions after the ceiling had been reached. In either case, future state reserves might not be available for benefits, and it would be inadvisable for a state to accumulate a reserve fund in a way that measurably increased the risk of insolvency in its federal trust fund account.

CONFORMITY ISSUES

The discussion to this point has assumed that that principal in a state's reserve fund goes solely toward UI benefit payments. However, there are no federal regulations governing this point. The use of state reserve fund assets is not subject to federal conformity review, either at the time the legislation is enacted or if the state brings in legislation to change the use.

It might be argued that the creation of a state reserve fund implies diverting some tax revenue from the federal trust fund to the state reserve fund and is, therefore, subject to federal conformity review; but creating a state reserve fund is a two-step process. First, the state levies a state reserve fund tax. Clearly, a state can levy any tax it chooses—no conformity issue here. Second, the state reduces the tax rate on UI taxes designated for the state's federal account—also perfectly within the bounds of conformity. Conformity requirements would have to be tied to the solvency of the state's federal trust fund. Staff at the Department of Labor have indicated it would be difficult to draft such a requirement, but the possibility should not be completely ruled out.

Given the lack of conformity requirements, the establishment of a state reserve fund could threaten the solvency of a state's federal trust fund and increase the need for future borrowing.[6] The legislation creating a reserve fund in a given state might be widely accepted if it were based on the premise that the fund would change the amount of money available for benefits but would generate extra revenue for state programs. However, a change in state government could lead to a change in policy and leave reserve fund assets vulnerable to a raid.

Thus far, conformity requires only that the reserve fund be completely separate from the state's federal UI account. For example, state reserves cannot enter into the calculation of an employer's UI tax rate. As shown in the case of Indiana's 1991 reserve fund deliberations, the requirement can be easily satisfied.

Whether a state may use federal administrative grants to cover the costs of collecting its reserve fund tax is not completely resolved. General Administration Letter 4-91 specifies that Title III grants can be used for the administration of taxes only to the extent that the associated revenue benefits the UI program. As noted, how a state's reserve fund assets might be used in the future remains unclear. A state might be tempted to use the fund's principal for a purpose other than paying UI benefits. If the federal government were to provide full administrative funding for state reserve fund tax collections, it would need to recover part of that administrative allocation if the state reserve fund were then used for a different purpose. On the other hand, if faced with a federal requirement to repay UI administrative grants, states might be less likely to change the uses of reserve fund assets.

FOUR STATE RESERVE FUNDS

The first state to create a reserve fund was North Carolina, in 1986. Its employers paid reserve fund taxes from 1987 to 1991. The principal in the reserve fund remained at about $200 million from 1992 through 1996. Interest from the fund is deposited into the state's Worker Training Trust Fund. Between 1992 and 1995, expenditures from the latter ranged from $12 to $14 million annually. The monies have been used mainly to finance ES program administration and job training. Other states with reserve funds have copied many features of North Carolina's legislation.

To highlight key aspects of state reserve funds, Table 5-1 compares funds across the four states that have created such funds. The Idaho, North Carolina, and Oregon reserve funds have met their target balances. Nebraska, which started to collect reserve fund taxes in 1996, expects to meet its target balance sometime between 1999 and 2001.

All four states finance the reserve fund by redirecting 20 percent of employer taxes from the state's UI account at the U.S. Treasury into a state account. This percentage was originally used in North Carolina and was copied by the other states. All four states also set a reserve fund ceiling of 1 percent of taxable wages. If the reserve fund exceeds this threshold on the computation date, the reserve fund tax is set at zero for the next year. In all but North Carolina, the tax continues to be collected in such years but is deposited in the state's U.S. Treasury account. North Carolina, in contrast, reduces total UI taxes by 20 percent in years that the reserve fund tax is not needed.[7]

The employer taxes that finance the reserve fund are levied at rates that reflect employers' experiences. After the taxes enter the reserve fund, however, they are commingled, so the fund does not record individual employers' contributions. In effect, reserve fund activities are financed by experience-rated taxes, not by flat-rate taxes. Flat-rate payroll taxes finance many state training funds, including California's Employment Training Panel.[8]

Table 5-1 Key Provisions of Reserve Funds in Four States

Provision	Idaho	Nebraska	North Carolina	Oregon
Size of UI tax redirection (%)	20	20	20	20
Reserve fund ceiling[a] (% of taxable wages)	1	1	1	1
Rediversion of taxes to U.S. Treasury after ceiling is reached?	Yes	Yes	No	Yes
Reserve fund principal dedicated to UI benefits?	Yes	Yes	Yes	Yes
Reserve fund interest earnings deposited into separate state fund?	Yes	Yes	Yes	Yes
Main use of state interest earnings				
Job training	X	X	X	X
Unemployment insurance administrative costs	X			X
Employment service administrative costs	X		X	X
Reserve fund administrative costs	X	X	X	X

[a] The computation used to deactivate the reserve fund tax also considers the balance in the state's federal trust fund account. In Nebraska, the reserve fund tax can also be deactivated if combined taxes would put employers in the lowest tax schedule.

All four states dedicate the principal in the reserve fund to the payment of UI benefits. Although the principal resides in the states, its uses are limited to making loans to the state's U.S. Treasury account, serving as collateral for FUA loans to the Treasury account, or repaying the principal and interest on Title XII loans. In years when part of the reserve fund's principal is on loan, less interest income will accrue to the state.

To establish clear accountability for the use of the reserve fund interest earnings, the four states have created separate trust funds to receive the interest earnings: the Special Administration Fund in Idaho, the Nebraska Training and Support Trust Fund, the Worker Training Trust Fund in North Carolina, and the Supplemental Administrative Fund in Oregon. Each fund issues an annual report.

The bottom rows of Table 5-1 show the main uses of reserve fund interest earnings. Each of the four states uses some monies to administer reserve fund taxes.[9] Nebraska, North Carolina, and Oregon finance worker training and skill-improvement programs with interest earnings. Reserve fund interest supplements the administrative budgets of the UI and/or ES programs in Idaho, North Carolina, and Oregon.

STATE EXPERIENCES WITH RESERVE FUNDS

State experiences with reserve funds have generally been satisfactory. This section briefly discusses these experiences but is restricted to a qualitative analysis.

While a state might be tempted to "raid" the principal in its reserve fund, there have been no major diversions to date.[10] However, concerns about the potential for raiding can never be fully allayed. The state law that created the reserve fund can be amended to divert some or all of the assets to other uses; this is a fact of state-level politics. To the extent that a state's finances deteriorate under continued pressures for low taxes, reserve funds could be tempting targets for raids.

The interest earnings of reserve funds are substantial. Once the funds reached their targets of 1 percent of taxable wages, fund investments in financial instruments yielding 6.0 to 7.0 percent have meant $12–14 million annually in North Carolina and Oregon and about

$3.0 million annually in Idaho. The annual interest yield is equivalent to a state payroll tax of 0.06 to 0.07 percent. This yield is similar to tax rates in Alabama, Georgia, Hawaii, Nevada, and South Carolina, where payroll taxes finance training and UI and/or ES administrations.

Holding assets in a derivative fund also provides a state with a margin for planning. Idaho, for example, has not spent all of its reserve fund interest but has reinvested the assets of its derivative administrative fund. This strategy partly reflects Idaho's concerns about future reductions in federal funding for UI and ES activities. Holding assets in an administrative fund gives Idaho the opportunity to offset federal funding reductions and maintain administration without immediately having to impose a new tax.[11]

North Carolina, Oregon, and Idaho, the three states with mature reserve funds, have seen reductions in their trust fund reserves held at the U.S. Treasury. From the end of 1989 to the end of 1996, North Carolina's federal balance declined from $1,471 million to $1,336 million. The associated reserve ratio multiple dropped from 1.26 to 0.77. When reserve fund balances are considered, the drop in North Carolina's total reserves over the same period was from $1,580 million to $1,536 million, and the reserve ratio multiple dropped from 1.35 to 0.89. In Idaho, the combined sum of federal plus state balances rose from $220 million at the end of 1989 to $323 million at the end of 1996. However, the combined reserve ratio multiple decreased from 1.37 to 1.15. Oregon's combined reserve ratio multiple decreased from 1.35 to 1.24 over the same period.[12]

All three states still had above-average reserve positions at the end of 1996, when the national reserve ratio multiple was 0.64. These states, even after declines in their combined trust fund reserve ratio multiples, did not face the threat of insolvency at the end of 1996. At the same time, the three used monies from state reserve fund interest for purposes not permitted for the interest earned on federal trust fund accounts.

An earlier report by Worden and Vroman (1991b) analyzed whether having a reserve fund increases a state's risk of insolvency. The analysis used a state-specific trust fund model to simulate reserve balances during various recessions. There is a slight increase in the risk of insolvency, which directly reflects the diversion of interest earnings from the state reserve fund. However, the report concluded that the increased risk of insolvency is very slight.

SUMMARY

A state's reserve fund interest can have a positive impact on that state's economy. When designing a reserve fund, a state needs to consider both the amount of interest income to be diverted and the implications that diverting that amount will have for the UI trust fund's solvency. The biggest threat to solvency comes not from the loss of interest earnings from the federal account but from diverting the reserve fund's principal to another state-funded activity. To date, this has not happened in any of the four states with reserve funds.

A state with a small federal trust fund account (for example, a reserve ratio multiple below 0.75) should not consider establishing a reserve fund. For a state with a small balance, the transition period (when employer taxes are partially diverted into the reserve fund) would further threaten the solvency of its federal trust fund account while generating insignificant state interest income.

If, however, the state reserve fund principal remains dedicated to paying UI benefits, the results of the simulation indicate a very slight increase in the risk of insolvency. This finding is logical, for the state would be, for the most part, merely shifting reserves from one location to another.

Notes

1. This chapter draws on a paper by Worden and Vroman (1991b).
2. Evaluations of reemployment programs in Illinois, New Jersey, and Washington suggest that paying reemployment bonuses may be a cost-effective way to reduce UI benefit payments. See Woodbury and Spiegelman (1987), Corson et al. (1989), and Spiegelman, O'Leary, and Kline (1992). There is less evidence about the effects of training and retraining on UI outlays.
3. Tax rates are slightly affected if interest income enters the reserve ratio computation, because part of total interest income is spent rather than being reinvested in the reserve fund.
4. The higher level could come about in two ways. First, if a second condition also had to be met, the balance would be higher than, say, 1 percent of wages and sala-

ries. For example, the state might also require that its federal balance equal a certain threshold before the reserve fund tax could be turned off. Second, if the state reserve fund made loans to the federal account and the ceiling were based on the total available reserves (state plus federal accounts), the state would continue to levy a reserve fund tax for more years, causing the reserve fund to reach a higher level.

5. Note that the amount of interest revenue lost to the federal trust fund would be greater than the sum of annual state reserve fund interest income drawn out of the system. State withdrawals do not reflect the lost compounding effects that would occur if all trust fund reserves were kept in the federal account. The size of this interest-on-interest loss is modest.

6. The threat of insolvency could also motivate states to enact legislation to restrict future UI benefits.

7. In all four states, the computation of the reserve fund tax also considers the balance in the state's federal trust fund account.

8. If a state intends to use its reserve fund interest earnings primarily to finance worker training, the distinction between a state reserve fund and other state payroll tax-financed training initiatives is not very sharp. A state facing reduced UI taxes because of experience-rating can limit the reduction by simultaneously imposing a training tax. This occurred in California when the Employment Training Panel was first established. Perhaps the crucial distinction has to do with the political environment at the time the state creates the fund. If a state wants to create a reserve fund but keep its UI tax rates stable, it must reduce its U.S. Treasury account. Otherwise, employer taxes will rise.

9. The Employment and Training Administration's General Administrative Letter 4-91 discusses the allocation of costs in states that levy both a reserve fund tax and regular UI taxes. However, some issues concerning the use of federal administrative grants to collect reserve fund taxes are not yet fully resolved. See U.S. Department of Labor, Employment and Training Administration (1991) for a discussion of those issues.

10. There were temporary diversions in North Carolina in the late 1980s, but both the principal and the associated interest were fully repaid.

11. Of course, a large reduction in federal funding would cause administrative fund assets to be quickly depleted. However, having such assets would give the state more time to decide how to respond to the reduced funding.

12. Note the balances for the federal accounts and associated reserve ratio multiples that appear in Table 1-4.

6 Conclusions

Overall, the fiscal strength of state UI programs at the end of 1996 was weaker than it had been at the end of 1989, just before the onset of the most recent recession. The national reserve ratio (high-cost) multiple dropped from 0.87 at the end of 1989 to 0.64 at the end of 1996. The economic recovery of the 1990s has lasted several years, and it appears that trust fund reserves will not be rebuilt to 1989 levels, or that rebuilding will occur slowly over many years. States are more at risk for insolvency in the late 1990s than they were in 1990. A repetition of widespread and large-scale borrowing of the past is a distinct possibility.

It might be argued that the states now have more flexible financing than they had two decades ago. However, the research summarized in Chapter 2 does not support such an assertion. UI programs continue to need to maintain large trust funds in anticipation of recessions.

The literature review in Chapter 2 cites only three studies on flexible financing. Clearly, more studies are required. Many states are likely to have low reserve positions for the immediate future (even without a recession in 1998 or 1999), making further study of flexible financing all the more important. Support from the U.S. Department of Labor on this important question would seem warranted.

States with indexed tax bases clearly show stronger trust fund positions than nonindexed states. Between 1986 and 1996, the indexed states maintained their taxable wage proportions and tax capacity, but nonindexed states had declines in both. During the next recession, it would be wise to note the borrowing patterns of states according to their indexing arrangements. It appears that the states most at risk of needing large loans are those with indexed maximum weekly benefits but nonindexed tax bases.

Three states compensate for UI trust fund indebtedness by issuing state debt instruments. The interest rates for such financial instruments were lower than for Title XII loans, but it is not clear that these states realized any savings on interest costs. For each of the three, the size of the state debt issue exceeded the amount needed for repaying Title XII loans. Each state later exercised call features for some of its long-term bonds. These issues were "too large" compared with Title XII loans, but to some degree that is inevitable, since the amount needed cannot be precisely known at the time a bond is issued. Moreover, the experiences with state bond issues to date represent only a sampling of the potential variety of future state debt issues.

For states with large trust fund balances, state reserve funds offer interesting potential. A state can use the interest earnings from state-held reserves for activities not permitted when reserves are held in accounts at the U.S. Treasury. The four states with reserve funds have financed worker training and UI and ES program administration through reserve fund interest earnings. Other states with healthy trust fund balances might want to consider following their example.

Financing UI programs will continue to be a challenge to the states, especially in an era of increasingly tight fiscal constraints. Undoubtedly, individual states will experiment with setting the minimum acceptable fund balance and with flexible financing. More research is needed on minimum adequate trust fund balances, UI tax responsiveness, and alternative borrowing arrangements for debtor states. If such research were done before the onset of the next recession, the findings could help states pass more easily through that recession.

The question of national leadership in defining and encouraging large state trust fund balances continues to be important. Publicizing state-level details about reserve adequacy (using standard indicators of adequacy such as the reserve ratio multiple) could be helpful. Providing financial rewards to states with large balances would seem useful. Such rewards could take the form of higher interest rate payments on balances above certain thresholds or reduced borrowing costs if pre-recession balances satisfied common actuarial thresholds. Federal leadership in this area could help to counter the political forces that advocate reducing UI taxes. Success in rebuilding and maintaining state trust fund balances would help UI programs better meet their traditional objectives: maintaining the incomes of households with unemployment and improving the built-in stability of the macroeconomy.

Appendix A

A Simulation Analysis of Potential Future Borrowing

A set of simulation projections helps to illustrate the risk of insolvency posed by low trust fund balances at the start of 1997. All projections are based on the state-level relationship between increases in unemployment and decreases in the reserve ratio multiple during 1990–1992. A cross-section regression with weighted state data was fitted to derive parameters for the relationship. The resulting equation was then used to project counterfactual trust fund drawdowns during 1990–1992 and 1997–1999. For both periods, initial reserve ratio multiples were noted and alternative recession-related drawdowns were simulated. The results show that many more states could need loans than the seven that actually borrowed during 1991–1995.

The cross-section regression, with states weighted by the size of their labor forces, was the following:

Eq. A1 $\text{RRM92} - \text{RRM89} = 0.3157 - 0.5526 \times (\text{TUR9092/TUR8789})$
$$(2.65) \quad (6.01)$$

Adj. $R^2 = 0.818$
Std. err. $= 0.249$

where RRM89 and RRM92 are the reserve ratio multiples, TUR9092 and TUR8789 are average unemployment rates for 1990–1992 and 1987–1989, and t ratios appear in parentheses beneath the coefficients.

The regression shows a strong statistical association between the two series, with larger decreases in reserve ratio multiples for states in which unemployment rate ratios were higher.

Chapter 1 notes that seven states needed U.S. Treasury loans during the 1991–1995 period. As shown in Table 1-4, Connecticut, Massachusetts, Michigan, and the District of Columbia had negative net balances at the end of 1992. Maine, New York, and Missouri had positive net balances at the end of 1992, even though they needed loans. Note, however, that the two states with large-scale borrowing during 1991–1994 (Connecticut and Massachusetts) had negative net reserves at the end of 1992, and their reserve ratio multiples were the most negative of all state-level multiples.

A simulation that projects reserve ratio multiples at the end of hypothetical recessions would not be expected to identify all states needing loans. Cash-flow loans would be expected for some states that ended the year with positive trust fund balances. Further, the simulations do not attempt to measure the size of loans to individual states. However, the simulations would be expected to identify states with substantial borrowing needs.

The simulations use actual reserve ratio multiples at the beginning of two hypothetical recessions which started at the end of 1989 and at the end of 1996. Reserve drawdowns then were simulated for three-year periods. Historic unemployment rate ratios were used along with Eq. A1 to project the size of the drawdowns. Subtracting the projected drawdown from the starting reserve ratio multiple yields the simulated multiple three years later.

Each state's actual unemployment experiences are included in the simulated trust fund drawdowns. There are four different recessions whose exact years are shown in Table 1-2. The number of states with negative end balances was then recorded for each of the four scenarios. The results for the 1990–1992 and the 1997–1999 periods differ due to differences in initial state trust fund balances. For the 1990–1992 recession, the number of states with negative balances at the end of 1992 ranged from 5 to 11. For the hypothetical 1997–1999 recession, the number of states with negative balances at the end of 1999 ranged from 7 to 17. Simulated borrowing was more widespread using recession-related unemployment rate ratios from (1981–1983/1977–1979) and (1971–1973/1967–1969) than using ratios from (1990–1992/1987–1989) and (1974–1976/1971–1973).

Two inferences may be drawn from the simulations.

1. That there were no widespread financing problems during 1990–1992 is attributable both to the mild nature of the recession and to the comparatively large initial trust fund balances held by the states. The states may not be as lucky in the next recession and may face increases in unemployment of much greater magnitude.

2. More states needed loans when they entered recessions with their 1996 reserves than with their 1989 reserves. Based on 1993–1996 rates of trust fund accumulation, several states will start the next recession with smaller balances than they had at the end of 1989. Other things being equal, these smaller balances will cause increased borrowing.

Appendix B

Analysis of Trust Fund Reserves
During Recessions

The cyclical importance of tax-base indexing is examined with data from the three most recent recessions. Three periods of recession-related draw-downs are examined: 1974–1976, 1981–1983, and 1990–1992. These three recessions were selected because each had a measurable number of states with indexed tax bases for at least part of the three-year period.[1] Changes in year-end reserve ratio multiples from the start to the end of the periods indicated were the dependent variables. To ensure that small states did not unduly influence the results, some regressions were fitted with data weighted by the size of each state's labor force (the 1976–1989 average).

The specifications use four independent variables:

1. The growth in the unemployment rate (TUR) was expected to exert a negative effect on the three-year change in reserve ratio multiples. This is measured as a ratio of the average TUR for the three years of heavy drawdowns to the average TUR for the three preceding years (for example, the 1990–1992 average TUR as a ratio to the 1987–1989 average).[2]

2. A dummy variable for the presence of an indexed maximum WBA was used. This variable measures the fraction of the three recession years when indexing was present and was expected to have a negative coefficient. Larger reductions in RRMs would be expected in states with indexed maximum WBAs, a reflection of continuing growth in the average WBA.

3. A dummy variable for tax-base indexing was also used, measured as the fraction of the three-year period that an indexed tax base was present. It was expected to have a positive coefficient, due to the automatic positive effect that an increased tax base has on tax revenues.

4. The level of the RRM at the start of the period was entered. It was expected that states with low initial RRMs might enact more legislation during recessions to avoid large-scale borrowing. This variable was expected to have a negative coefficient, that is, larger reductions in RRMs in states where RRMs were initially higher. Unfortunately, there is also an econometric reason to expect a negative coefficient

for this variable. Since the lagged RRM is part of the dependent variable with a negative sign of –1.0, the measurement also leads to an expected negative sign for the lagged RRM. Because the interpretation of a negative coefficient is ambiguous, results are shown both with and without the lagged RRM.

Table B-1 displays 12 regressions, the product of three recessions, two specifications, and two weighting schemes for the state-level data. All regressions are based on the 50 states plus the District of Columbia. Overall, the equations produce several of the expected results, with adjusted R^2 values of from 0.34 to 0.63 in unweighted data and from 0.70 to 0.92 in weighted data. Generally, the four variables enter with the expected signs, and the majority of coefficients are significant at the 0.05 or 0.01 level.[3]

In each regression, the unemployment ratio enters with the expected negative sign and its coefficient consistently has the largest t ratio. Note that the TUR ratio coefficients are largest for 1973–1976, intermediate for 1980–1983, and smallest for 1989–1992. Higher unemployment rate ratios are associated with bigger trust fund drawdowns. However, the size of the effect was considerably smaller for 1989–1992 than for 1973–1976.

Both indexing variables usually enter with the expected signs. The presence of an indexed maximum WBA enters negatively in eight of 12 regressions, but the indexed tax base enters positively in all 12. Note, however, that the indexed maximum positive coefficient is significant in weighted data.

All 12 of the tax-base indexing coefficients are positive; eight are significant at either the 0.01 or the 0.05 level, and a ninth just fails to be significant at the 0.05 level. The size of the coefficients for the 1973–1976 data seems surprising in light of the small number of states with tax-base indexing during those years. For 10 equations, the dummy variable coefficient lies in the range of 0.26 to 0.54.

The lagged RRM variable enters negatively and significantly in the first two recessions, but its coefficient is essentially zero for the most recent recession. That the coefficients for the lagged RRM and for the indexing of the maximum WBA both change size sharply for the 1990–1992 downturn suggests a changed pattern of inter-correlation between the two variables. However, there is no obvious explanation for the changed coefficients for this period.

The size of the dummy coefficients strongly suggests that tax-base indexing contributes to maintaining trust fund balances during recessions. These coefficients consistently fall within a narrow range, especially in the weighted data, and suggest a measurably positive effect on trust fund balances.

While such a finding is plausible, a comment made in Chapter 3 bears repeating: states with indexed tax bases may generally take a more proactive approach to trust fund management. Even so, the regressions suggest that tax-base indexing helps to maintain trust fund balances during recessions.

Notes

1. Two states had indexed tax bases in 1974, 6 in 1976, 13 in 1981, 14 in 1983, 18 in 1990, and 18 in 1992.
2. For the 1981–1983 period, the ratio was the average TUR for 1981–1983 divided by the average TUR for 1977–1979. This period had two recessions, with the first starting in 1980, but the TURs were highest in 1982 and 1983.
3. Under a one-sided test, the t ratio needs to be 1.68 to be significant at the 0.05 level and 2.41 to be significant at the 0.01 level.

Table B-1 Regressions Explaining Recession-Related Changes in Trust Fund Reserve Ratio Multiples[a]

Change in year-end RRM	Constant	TUR ratio	Max. WBA indexed (Yes=1)	Tax base indexed (Yes=1)	Lagged RRM	Summary Statistics		
						Adj. R^2	Standard error	Mean dependent variable
Unweighted data								
1973–1976	1.231 (3.41)	-1.675 (6.75)	-0.188 (1.45)	0.366 (1.66)		0.485	0.410	-1.054
1973–1976	1.277 (4.21)	-1.348 (6.11)	-0.186 (1.71)	0.061 (0.31)	-0.343 (4.54)	0.636	0.344	-1.054
1980–1983	0.945 (3.47)	-0.864 (4.87)	-0.216 (1.66)	0.014 (0.10)		0.341	0.389	-0.456
1980–1983	1.031 (4.26)	-0.792 (5.02)	-0.357 (2.96)	0.189 (1.39)	-0.311 (3.76)	0.485	0.344	-0.456
1989–1992	0.241 (2.36)	-0.418 (5.47)	0.007 (0.10)	0.167 (2.38)		0.441	0.211	-0.192
1989–1992	0.217 (1.62)	-0.418 (5.42)	0.015 (0.20)	0.157 (1.97)	0.025 (0.29)	0.430	0.213	-0.192
Weighted data								
1973–1976	0.971 (4.26)	-1.451 (8.35)	-0.182 (2.04)	0.543 (2.84)		0.899	0.346	-1.044
1973–1976	0.877 (4.18)	-1.148 (6.24)	-0.241 (2.90)	0.324 (1.74)	-0.252 (3.25)	0.916	0.316	-1.044

1980–1983	0.631	−0.746	−0.288	0.478		0.703	0.439	−0.514
	(2.88)	(4.47)	(2.64)	(2.23)				
1980–1983	1.039	−0.858	−0.565	0.501	−0.355	0.814	0.348	−0.514
	(5.48)	(6.42)	(5.63)	(2.95)	(5.39)			
1989–1992	0.155	−0.483	0.129	0.221		0.875	0.206	−0.289
	(1.34)	(5.81)	(2.81)	(2.76)				
1989–1992	0.207	−0.489	0.108	0.250	−0.049	0.873	0.208	−0.289
	(1.27)	(5.76)	(1.65)	(2.44)	(0.46)			

SOURCE: Data on reserve ratio multiples (RRMs), indexed maximum weekly benefit amounts (WBAs), and indexed tax bases are from the UI Service. Data on unemployment rates (TURs) are from the Bureau of Labor Statistics.

[a] Both indexation variables are measured as the fraction of the three years that indexing was in effect. TUR ratios are measured as ratios of three-year averages. All regressions are based on 50 states plus the District of Columbia. Beneath each coefficient is the absolute value of its t ratio.

References

Advisory Council on Unemployment Compensation. 1995. *Unemployment Insurance in the United States: Benefits, Financing and Coverage.* Washington, D.C.: Advisory Council on Unemployment Compensation.

Corson, Walter, et al. 1989. *New Jersey Unemployment Insurance Reemployment Demonstration Project.* UI Occasional Paper 89-3. Washington, D.C.: U.S. Department of Labor.

Haber, William, and Merrill Murray. 1966. *Unemployment Insurance in the American Economy.* Homewood, Illinois: Richard D. Irwin.

Miller, Mike, Robert Pavosevich, and Wayne Vroman. 1997. "Trends in Unemployment Benefit Financing." In *Unemployment Insurance in the United States: Analysis of Policy Issues*, Christopher J. O'Leary and Stephen J. Wandner, eds. Kalamazoo, Michigan: W.E. Upjohn Institute for Employment Research, pp. 365–421.

National Foundation for Unemployment Compensation and Workers' Compensation. 1996. *Highlights of State Unemployment Compensation Laws.* Washington, D.C.: National Foundation for Unemployment Compensation and Workers' Compensation.

National Foundation for Unemployment Compensation and Workers' Compensation. 1986. *Highlights of State Unemployment Compensation Laws.* Washington, D.C.: National Foundation for Unemployment Compensation and Workers' Compensation.

Spiegelman, Robert, Christopher O'Leary, and Kenneth Kline. *The Washington Reemployment Bonus Experiment Final Report.* 1992. Unemployment Insurance Occasional Paper No. 92-6. Washington, D.C.: U.S. Department of Labor.

U.S. Department of Labor, Employment and Training Administration. 1991. *Allocation of Costs of Assessing and Collecting State Taxes.* General Administration Letter No. 4-91, Washington, D.C.: U.S. Department of Labor.

U.S. Department of Labor, Employment and Training Administration. 1988. *Payment of Interest on Title XII Loans.* Unemployment Insurance Program Letter No. 58-88. Washington, D.C.: U.S. Department of Labor.

U.S. Department of Labor, Employment and Training Administration. 1995. "Unemployment Insurance Financial Data." *ET Handbook 394.* Washington D.C.: U.S. Department of Labor.

U.S. Department of Labor, Unemployment Insurance Service. 1996. *Comparison of State Unemployment Insurance Laws.* Washington, D.C.: U.S. Department of Labor.

U.S. Department of Labor, Unemployment Insurance Service. 1975. *Comparison of State Unemployment Insurance Laws*. Washington, D.C.: U.S. Department of Labor.

U.S. Department of Labor, Unemployment Insurance Service. 1966. *Comparison of State Unemployment Insurance Laws*. Washington, D.C.: U.S. Department of Labor.

Vroman, Wayne. 1996. *An Analysis of Unemployment Insurance Experience Rating: Draft Report*. Report to the U.S. Department of Labor, December.

———. 1993. *Alternatives for Financing Unemployment Insurance Trust Fund Debts: Final Report*. Report to the U.S. Department of Labor, July.

———. 1986. *The Funding Crisis in State Unemployment Insurance*. Kalamazoo, Michigan: W.E. Upjohn Institute for Employment Research, 199 pp.

———. 1990. *Unemployment Insurance Trust Fund Adequacy in the 1990s*. Kalamazoo, Michigan: W.E. Upjohn Institute for Employment Research, 176 pp.

Ward, Sally A. 1987. Testimony before the Subcommittee on Public Assistance and Unemployment Compensation of the Committee on Ways and Means, U.S. House of Representatives, Serial 100-46: 96–106.

Woodbury, Stephen, and Robert Spiegelman. 1987. "Bonuses to Workers and Employers to Reduce Unemployment: Randomized Trials in Illinois." *American Economic Review* (September): 513–530.

Worden, Kelleen, and Wayne Vroman. 1991a. *Solvency Provisions in State Unemployment Insurance Laws*. Washington, D.C.: The Urban Institute.

———. 1991b. *State Reserve Funds: An Idea for the 1990s*. Washington, D.C.: The Urban Institute.

Author Index

Subject Index

About the Institute

The W. E. Upjohn Institute for Employment Research is a nonprofit research organization devoted to finding and promoting solutions to employment-related problems at the national, state, and local levels. It is an activity of the W. E. Upjohn Unemployment Trustee Corporation, which was established in 1932 to administer a fund set aside by the late Dr. W. E. Upjohn, founder of The Upjohn Company, to seek ways to counteract the loss of employment income during economic downturns.

The Institute is funded largely by income from the W. E. Upjohn Unemployment Trust, supplemented by outside grants, contracts, and sales of publications. Activities of the Institute comprise the following elements: 1) a research program conducted by a resident staff of professional social scientists; 2) a competitive grant program, which expands and complements the internal research program by providing financial support to researchers outside the Institute; 3) a publications program, which provides the major vehicle for disseminating the research of staff and grantees, as well as other selected works in the field; and 4) an Employment Management Services division, which manages most of the publicly funded employment and training programs in the local area.

The broad objectives of the Institute's research, grant, and publication programs are to 1) promote scholarship and experimentation on issues of public and private employment and unemployment policy, and 2) make knowledge and scholarship relevant and useful to policymakers in their pursuit of solutions to employment and unemployment problems.

Current areas of concentration for these programs include causes, consequences, and measures to alleviate unemployment; social insurance and income maintenance programs; compensation; workforce quality; work arrangements; family labor issues; labor-management relations; and regional economic development and local labor markets.

W.E. UPJOHN
INSTITUTE

0-88099-193-3